VEGETARIAN BURGERS

1. 00

VEGETARIAN BURGERS

Bharti Kirchner

HarperPerennial
A Division of HarperCollins*Publishers*

HarperCollins books may be purchased
for educational, business, or sales
promotional use. For information please write:
Special Markets Department, HarperCollins
Publishers, Inc., 10 East 53rd Street, New York,
NY 10022.

FIRST EDITION

Designed by Stephanie Tevonian

ISBN 0–06–095115–X

96 97 98 99 00 ❖/RRD 10 9 8 7 6 5 4 3 2 1

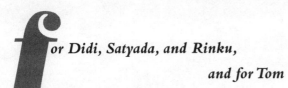

or Didi, Satyada, and Rinku,

and for Tom

ACKNOWLEDGMENTS

*To all those who encouraged me,
criticized my writing, and sampled my
dishes: You know who you are.*

Thank you!

CONTENTS

INTRODUCTION
THE ALL-AMERICAN BURGER
GOES VEGETARIAN

*i*n recent years vegetarian burgers have become a passion for me. I believe this to be a result of living in the United States, where a meal on a bun with all the trimmings is a way of life. I use a wealth of nuts, seeds, whole grains, legumes, vegetables, and spices to produce exciting, nutritionally sound vegetarian burgers. They are not difficult to prepare, requiring only a food processor.

I was introduced to vegetarian patties as a child in India, the land of my birth, where meat eaters and vegetarians have influenced each other's cooking for thousands of years. Indian cooks prepare not only many sorts of ground meat patties, called *kebabs*, but they also do an equally varied set of vegetable patties, known as *chop, patis, tikki,* or *bora.*

These vegetarian delights are composed of legumes, grains, and various minced vegetables, laced with fresh chiles, herbs, and spices. Indian cooks roll them into balls or flatten them into oval shapes, then coat them with bread crumbs before frying or baking. In India they are not served on a bun. Rather, they are accompanied by rice, flat bread, lentil stew, chutney, and fresh chile slivers for a well-rounded meal.

Middle Eastern cooks produce such burgerlike preparations as falafel and kibbe. They combine minced vegetables and meat with grains, nuts, and spices, which are formed into cakes or balls that are fried or baked, then served with a variety of accompaniments including raw onion and spiced yogurt. Their custom of adding pine nuts and cracked wheat to the burger mixture inspired several recipes in this book.

Additional burger ideas came to me while traveling in Europe and Asia. Kasha, also known as buckwheat, blends smoothly with

1

walnuts and lima beans to create a rich burger. Indian basmati rice mixed with velvety Japanese shiitake mushrooms and formed into a burger is sensational. Swiss chard has a special affinity for the Korean seasonings of soy sauce, sesame oil, and garlic that, in combination with mushrooms, yields a burger with outstanding flavor and a high nutritional profile. Tofu burgers are nothing new, but smoking tofu in a burner-top smoker imparts a rich, earthy taste that brings the romance of open-fire cooking to the vegetarian table. For variety, I also stuff the burgers Indian style, filling their centers with sweet onion, hard-cooked eggs, or wilted greens.

Friends who describe commercial vegetarian burgers as "a bit bland" are pleasantly surprised by these innovations. Even meat-eating friends find these vegetarian burgers to be a pleasant change of pace. In the recipes that follow I introduce the Western palate to many exciting new tastes.

In keeping with current nutritional guidelines, I have worked to reduce fat and cholesterol content. Grilling, baking, or broiling are my primary methods of cooking, and sautéing is an alternative. The use of eggs or dairy products is, for the most part, optional. This makes these burgers acceptable to "vegans," those vegetarians who shun all animal products.

Most of the recipes are simple and the majority of the ingredients are now available in supermarkets. Leftover cooked grains, beans, and vegetables can be cleverly turned into burgers, and many of the steps can be done ahead of time. What's more, these low-fat patties can be frozen.

By varying the side dishes and trimmings, one can be sure that these versatile burgers are seldom served the same way twice. The American style of presentation with "the works" has flair and is part of the attraction. But these burgers can also be paired with a rice pilaf, wrapped in a chapati with chutney, or slipped into a pita pocket with a spicy salsa, creating a whole different dining experience. Surrounded by imaginative side dishes, the humble vegetarian burger becomes a gourmet treat appropriate at an elegant luncheon or simply for entertaining that special vegetarian guest.

Condiments are essential to the enjoyment of vegetarian burgers, so I have dedicated an entire chapter to quick salsas, flavorful chutneys, fiery sambals, and relishes from around the world. All have been selected for their affinity with vegetarian burgers. Another chapter features a few select side dishes that promise to make these burgers even more satisfying and pleasurable.

I feel that these richly flavored and highly nutritious patties should be in the repertoire of all cooks—carnivores and vegetarians alike. Try these recipes. Use the many tips. And, by all means, create variations of your own by venturing beyond.

TOOLS

A *food processor* is a must for preparing vegetarian burgers. It helps blend the ingredients, creates the proper texture, and eliminates the need for eggs as a binding agent. Any simple processor with attachments for grating or shredding will do the job; a fancy machine is not necessary.

Alternatively, you can use a food mill, mortar, or, in some cases, a potato masher. This will, however, lengthen the preparation time and create a coarser mixture that doesn't bind as well. In this case, consider adding one whole egg or two egg whites to be sure that the burgers will retain their shape.

Don't substitute a blender for a food processor. Most blenders will not grind the ingredients properly without requiring extra liquid. This, in turn, will make the mixture too soft and runny to be formed into patties.

An electric *spice/coffee grinder* is ideal for pulverizing small amounts of nuts or seeds to a powdered form. You can also use a blender or food processor, but the food can stick to the sides, making it difficult to extract. Note that it is preferable to have a separate grinder for this purpose, as the gadget can't be used to grind coffee after you've ground other foods in it.

For grilling burgers, a *vegetable grid* works best. They come in many varieties. My favorite is a flat metal sheet made of heavy gauge steel with a nonstick surface and a pattern of evenly spaced holes, approximately ¼ inch in diameter, that fits neatly on top of a grill. Even the most tender and fragile foods can be grilled on this grid without falling into the fire. You can also use a *hinged basket*, a two-sided hinged grill with long handles that encloses one or more patties, depending on size. They are especially useful for delicate burgers, enabling them to be turned and moved around the grill without fear of breakage. If sautéing, use a *nonstick skillet* and *nonstick spatula* for turning the burgers.

INGREDIENTS

The ingredients below are available in supermarkets, natural food shops, and Asian, Indian, or Latin American specialty food shops.

ASAFETIDA. A brown resinous compound from India with a strong garlicky flavor, sold in rocklike chunks or fine powder. If you have purchased the chunk form, simply break off a piece and grind it in a mortar or spice grinder. The powder is more convenient.

BLACK SALT. This salt from India is grayish pink in color, not black. It has a distinctive flavor and adds an earthy touch to condiments.

BULGUR (CRACKED WHEAT). Hulled wheat, parboiled, then dried and coarsely ground; available in fine, medium, or coarse textures. For the recipes in this book, use fine cracked wheat. You can also use packaged tabbouleh mix if the seasoning has not been premixed with the cracked wheat.

CARAWAY. Small, brown, crescent-shaped seeds, these add a pleasant, sweet taste to grains and vegetables.

CHIPOTLE CHILE. Dried and smoked jalapeños from Mexico. They have a wonderfully smoky flavor, but are extremely hot, so use a small amount initially, then adjust to your taste.

CUMIN. Cumin comes both whole and ground. The whole seeds resemble caraway and have a pleasantly bitter taste. Ground cumin is strongly aromatic.

GARAM MASALA. This mixture of "hot" spices from India is dominated by ground cinnamon, cardamom, and cloves. Garam masala gives a fragrant spicy flavor to vegetarian burgers.

HOISIN SAUCE. A thick, spicy-sweet paste from China, favored as a dip. Rich brown in color, it's made primarily with fermented soybeans and garlic.

KASHA (BUCKWHEAT GROATS). In Eastern Europe kasha denotes any grain-based porridge, but in the United States it refers specifically to buckwheat groats, which are not a grain but, rather, the seeds of the buckwheat plant. Buckwheat groats have a delightful nutty flavor and a crunchy texture; they are cooked like a grain.

MILLET. This tiny, delicate grain becomes light and fluffy when cooked and can form the foundation for vegetarian burgers. Whole millet can be pressed into the surface of burgers to provide textural variety and visual appeal.

MUSTARD SEEDS. In these recipes I use black mustard seeds (also called brown mustard seeds), which are smaller and more flavorful than the common yellow variety.

QUINOA. A tiny beige grain, similar to millet but smaller, with a very high protein content. Important: Rinse several times before using to remove a naturally occurring bitter residue, saponin.

SAMBAL OELEK. A red chile paste used as a seasoning or as an accompaniment. It is flavorful, but extremely hot, so use in small amounts.

SESAME OIL. In these recipes I use the strong, nutty flavored dark sesame oil available in Asian markets. Don't substitute light sesame oil sold in supermarkets and natural food stores.

SESAME SEEDS. These small oval seeds are used whole or ground and impart a nutty flavor to burgers.

SHISO (PERILLA). Also known as beefsteak plant. The spicy pungent leaves, either green or purple, have earthy overtones and can be used raw or cooked.

TAMARI. This by-product of miso (a fermented soybean paste) resembles soy sauce, but has a deeper flavor and holds up better under intense heat. If it is available, buy the low-sodium variety.

TAMARIND. Refers to the dried pulp of the tamarind fruit, which has a complex, tart taste. It is sold either in jars of ready-to-use concentrate or compressed cakes of the whole fruit, which must be pitted and soaked in hot water before using. The recipes in this book call for the more convenient ready-to-use concentrate.

TEMPEH. Tempeh is a flat fermented soybean cake with a musky, nutty taste. It's rich in protein and one of the few vegetable sources of vitamin B_{12}.

TOFU (BEAN CURD). Milky white, custard-like cake derived from soybean milk.

TURMERIC. Dried ground turmeric, a bright yellow powder, is derived from the roots of a plant in the ginger family. It adds a warm, faintly bitter taste and yellow highlight to dishes.

VEGETARIAN OYSTER SAUCE. The vegetarian equivalent of Chinese oyster sauce is made of soybeans and mushroom extract. It's not widely available yet, but worth looking for.

TECHNIQUES

PEELING AND/OR SEEDING TOMATOES

To peel tomatoes, plunge them into boiling water for approximately 1 minute or until their skins split. Remove from heat and cool to room temperature. Peel, discard the skins, and squeeze out the seeds. Place the flesh and juices in a bowl and chop the flesh coarsely.

Some recipes call for unpeeled, seeded tomatoes. To seed an unpeeled tomato, cut it in half crosswise and squeeze out the seeds or scoop them out using a teaspoon.

PREPARING BREAD CRUMBS

Most vegetarian burger recipes call for bread crumbs. They are available in supermarkets, but can also be prepared at home to ensure freshness. By varying the type of bread, you can come up with different flavor variations. Rye, multigrain, and Italian rustic breads are among the many possibilities.

Cut 8 slices of bread into 1-inch cubes and arrange in a single layer on an ungreased baking sheet. Bake in a 350-degree oven for 15 to 20 minutes or until the cubes are thoroughly dry and their tops turn medium brown. Grind them to a coarse powder in a blender or food processor. Stored in the refrigerator in a tightly sealed container, they maintain their freshness for several days. You can also freeze them. Makes about 1½ cups.

➤ **TWICE-BAKED BREAD CRUMBS:** Browning the bread crumbs above in the oven before using give them a richer, more roasted flavor. This is also a way of refreshing bread crumbs several days old. Spread the crumbs in a thin layer on an ungreased baking sheet. Bake in a 350-degree oven for about 10 minutes or until the crumbs turn light to medium brown in color. Watch carefully for signs of burning. (If the bread crumbs are stale, toasting will not rid them of the taste.)

➤ **WHEAT-FREE BREAD CRUMBS:** If you are wheat-sensitive, you can substitute a wheat-free bread, such as a brown rice or tapioca loaf, for preparing bread crumbs. Follow the method above, using a bread of your choice. These crumbs are more delicate and the resulting burgers may be slightly more fragile, so handle them gently.

PREPARING BULGUR

Bulgur (cracked wheat) adds bulk, absorbs moisture, and helps bind burgers. It needs to be soaked before using to soften it.

Soak ½ cup bulgur in 1 cup water for 30 to 40 minutes. By this time most of the water will be absorbed and the grains will swell. Makes just over 1 cup.

If a recipe calls for only ½ cup prepared bulgur, start with ¼ cup uncooked bulgur and ½ cup water and follow the above method.

RECONSTITUTING DRIED MUSHROOMS

To reconstitute dried mushrooms, soak them in warm water for 30 minutes or until they are soft and pliable. They will regain much of their flavor and texture and may be used like fresh mushrooms in cooking. The soaking water can also be used. If you are concerned about sediment, or if there are specks of matter in the soaking water, simply pour the water through a strainer or layers of cheesecloth.

TOASTING NUTS AND SEEDS

Toasting improves the flavor of nuts and seeds and also makes them easier to grind if they are to be used in powdered form. Place on an ungreased griddle or skillet over medium-low heat. Stir frequently for even roasting and allow them to turn light to medium brown. Remove from heat at this point, as most nuts and seeds burn easily. Watch for any signs of smoking or a burnt smell in the air. If this occurs they are already overdone and will have a slightly bitter flavor. Stored in the refrigerator in a covered container, toasted nuts or seeds retain their freshness for several weeks. You can also freeze them.

TIPS

THE LOW-FAT, LOW-CHOLESTEROL WAY

In these recipes, I use minimum oil and specify butter and eggs only as an option. The significant source of fat in most recipes is nuts or seeds, which are added for richness and texture. If you like, you can substitute bread crumbs for any portion of the amount of nuts or seeds called for in the recipes. This will slightly alter the final taste, but the result will still be quite acceptable.

A WORD ABOUT MEASUREMENTS

In order for the burgers to hold their shape, it is necessary to use precise amounts of the main ingredients. When cooked, the same grain or bean, originating from different sources, can yield widely varying amounts. For this reason, I specify a quantity of these ingredients that, when precooked, is guaranteed to produce the amount called for in the recipes. In many cases, this will result in a surplus that can be retained for use in other dishes.

MAKING VEGETARIAN BURGERS

To make a hamburger, the meat must first be ground. To make a vegetarian burger the ingredients must also be ground before they can be shaped into round patties. Bread crumbs are added to bind the ingredients together so that they will hold their shape during cooking. The optional use of a whole egg or egg whites not only enriches the flavor but also provides additional high-quality protein and other nutrients. The egg also functions as a binding agent in a manner similar to bread crumbs, but is moister.

If the vegetarian burgers are a little crumbly, make them firmer by including extra bread crumbs. In most recipes, up to an additional ½ cup of bread crumbs is specified as optional. Use this extra amount with care, adding a little bit at a time until the desired texture is achieved. As additional bread crumbs are used, the burger mixture will be easier to handle, but will become drier in the process.

Vegetarian burgers are flexible. They can be made into many shapes other than the standard hamburger patty. Try forming them into ovals, squares, or even sausage shapes, especially if you happen to be using baguettes or hot dog buns. The burger mixture can be optionally baked as a *vegetarian loaf*, then sliced and served sandwich-style or as an entrée just as you would a traditional meat loaf. And, as with hamburgers, a vegetarian burger can be transformed into a *patty melt*. Yet another alternative is the *vegetarian hot "beef" sandwich*. I have provided instructions for all three.

ADVANCE PREPARATION

For convenience, prepare the ingredients ahead of time. Grind the nuts. Make the bread crumbs, if you are starting from scratch. Cook the grains, beans, and vegetables. Form the patties early on the day you intend to serve them or even a day ahead of time. If preparing them more than an hour in advance, refrigerate them, then bring them to room temperature just prior to cooking.

FREEZING VEGETARIAN BURGERS

You can make a large batch of burgers by doubling or tripling the recipes and freezing the surplus. Wrap uncooked patties individually in plastic wrap. To thaw, transfer them to the refrigerator a day in advance.

COOKING METHODS

The burgers in this book can be broiled under the broiler or grilled over a charcoal, gas, or electric grill. In some recipes, sautéing is an option.

➤ **GRILLING OR BROILING INSTRUCTIONS:** If using an outdoor charcoal grill, be sure to let the charcoal briquettes burn until they are covered with a thin layer of gray ash with a dull red glow underneath. It generally takes about 30 minutes to reach this stage.

For a tantalizing smoky aroma and flavor, sprinkle the coals with hickory, mesquite, or other flavored wood chips that have been soaked in water. Grill burgers 3 to 5 inches from the heat source, otherwise they are likely to burn.

If broiling, do so also 3 to 5 inches from the heat. Each recipe specifies an approximate cooking time, but you will need to monitor the process to avoid overcooking.

➤ **SAUTÉING INSTRUCTIONS:** Sautéing helps retain the moistness of the burgers, but adds to their fat content. I haven't included sautéing instructions in every recipe, but any burger can be sautéed. Be sure to use a nonstick skillet and a nonstick spatula. Burgers that are fragile may be difficult to turn over, so coat these with extra bread crumbs before sautéing.

TOASTING THE BREAD

If you are using a grill, the bread or buns can be toasted alongside the burgers, if there is room. Cook the buns, cut side down, until golden brown. You can also grill tortillas or chapatis, but briefly—too long and they will become brittle and crumbly. Alternatively, heat the bread in a 450-degree oven for 5 minutes or just until warm and toasty.

SERVING VEGETARIAN BURGERS

You can serve vegetarian burgers the traditional way on a bun with all the trimmings. Or, you can be adventurous and experiment with the assortment of breads that are available. Dense coarse-textured breads such as Italian peasant bread, sourdough baguettes, or English muffins hold the traditional trimmings well.

Pita pockets are ideal for tucking in a vegetarian burger. Or, you might roll a burger up in a flat bread such as tortilla, chapati, or naan. In this case, make the burgers a bit smaller or, better yet, form them into "sausages." If using a flat bread, assemble the burgers just before serving, making sure there are no tears through which condiments might leak.

For variety, I offer suggestions on serving vegetarian burgers as an entrée, teamed with side dishes of grains and vegetables rather than bread. Try serving them in this manner to fully enjoy the flavor of these burgers without the trappings of traditional condiments.

To complement the taste and texture of vegetarian burgers, include at least one seasonal fresh fruit or vegetable. There are suggestions with each recipe, but the possibilities are endless.

FOR PICNICS

If picnicking, carry the bread, burgers, sliced vegetables, and condiments in separate containers and let the guests come up with their own combinations. This is especially effective with pita or other flat breads, which become soggy if filled ahead of time. The burgers can be reheated over the picnic grill or they can be served at room temperature.

REHEATING BURGERS

To reheat, place burgers in a 325-degree oven for up to 15 minutes or until thoroughly heated. Overbaking makes them dry.

A WORD ABOUT RECIPE NAMES

The recipe names emphasize one or more ingredients, depending on their relative importance. Since the ingredients are puréed first, you'll not always be able to distinguish a particular item by taste. But be aware that all the ingredients contribute to the final taste and texture.

A VEGETARIAN BURGER BY ANY OTHER NAME

Please note that I have used the terms "burger," "vegetarian burger," and "patty" interchangeably.

GRAIN AND BEAN BURGERS

EARTHY BURGERS WITH BUTTERY BEANS   18

FALAFEL BURGERS   20

CURRIED KIDNEY BEAN BURGERS   22

QUINOA AND BLACK BEAN BURGERS   24

REFRIED BEAN BURGERS WITH CHIPOTLE PEPPER   26

RED LENTIL AND MILLET BURGERS   28

ice and beans are among my favorite foods. Not only is each delicious in its own right, but taken together, they provide complete protein. One day, I puréed the two together, then dressed them with soy sauce and crushed hazelnuts before forming them into patties. The result had an altogether new taste—robust, yet refined.

Transformed this way, the grain-and-bean amalgam provided a whole new eating experience and set me on the path to writing this chapter.

Since then I have worked with many other grains such as quinoa, bulgur, and barley, and paired them with legumes of different types such as lentils, chick-peas, lima beans, and kidney beans. Grains bind the mixture and legumes improve the texture of the burgers.

For enhanced taste, I choose from an assortment of spices and flavorings. When using an assertive ingredient like kasha or black beans, I pick an equally bold condiment like sambal oelek or a spice mix like hot curry powder. When working with delicately fragrant basmati rice, I find a hint of fresh ginger to be more appropriate.

For those in search of meat substitutes, grain-and-bean burgers are a good source of protein. Many of these burgers incorporate one or more vegetable ingredients to further enhance their nutritional value.

Another advantage of grain-and-bean burgers is convenience. Leftovers such as millet, pinto beans, or wild rice are frequent burger components in my kitchen. If you are starting from scratch, these ingredients can be easily prepared a day ahead of time and stored in the refrigerator.

One way of making these burgers even more exciting is by accompanying them with sauces or spreads. I make some sauces using fresh seasonal fruits and vegetables, and others with richly spiced yogurt or buttermilk. These are the vegetarian versions of the traditional trimmings served with hamburgers, adding both flavor and visual appeal to the main attraction.

With such a rich array of grains, beans, fruits, vegetables, herbs, and spices from around the world, one need never be bored with vegetarian burgers. Each meal can be a new and exciting experience, limited only by one's own imagination.

EARTHY BURGERS WITH BUTTERY BEANS

*t*hese robust burgers composed of earthy kasha, buttery lima
beans, and rich-tasting walnuts have a smooth, delicate texture.
They are especially tasty served on onion rolls with maple mustard
and wine-glazed mushrooms.

Makes 6 to 8 patties, 3 to 4 servings

1 cup medium kasha
(buckwheat groats)
1 tablespoon olive oil
1 cup diced onion
1 tablespoon minced garlic
(see Note)
1 jalapeño pepper or other
green chile of choice,
cored, seeded, and minced
(or to taste)
¼ pound fresh mushrooms,
sliced ¼ inch thick
1 cup cooked or canned lima
(butter) beans
2 tablespoons ketchup
½ cup toasted walnut halves,
ground in a spice/coffee
grinder to a coarse powder

1¾ cups Bread Crumbs
(page 7) or commercial
bread crumbs
Salt and freshly ground
black pepper

CONDIMENT SUGGESTIONS
(Choose from one or more
of the following):
Fresh chopped arugula
Peeled, sliced cucumbers
Maple Mustard (page 111)
Wine-glazed Mushrooms
(page 101)

GARNISH (OPTIONAL)
Carrot curls

❶ Toast the kasha lightly in a saucepan by placing it over
medium-low heat until slightly darkened, stirring often. Add
2¼ cups water and bring to a boil. Reduce heat. Simmer, covered,
until all water is absorbed and kasha is light and fluffy, 10 to 15
minutes. Allow to cool to room temperature.
❷ Heat the olive oil in a medium skillet. Cook the onion and
garlic until the onion is wilted and the garlic is golden. Add the

jalapeño and the mushrooms and cook, uncovered, until softened, about 5 minutes, stirring every now and then. Remove from heat and allow to cool.

❸ Place kasha, mushroom-onion mixture, lima beans, and ketchup in the container of a food processor. Pulse on and off several times until the mixture is thoroughly blended. Transfer to a large bowl. Add the ground walnuts and 1 cup of the bread crumbs and season to taste with salt and pepper. Mix with a large spoon or, even better, with your hands, until all ingredients are thoroughly combined. Form into 3-inch patties ½ inch thick, mixing in extra bread crumbs if the patties don't hold their shape. They will be delicate, so handle them gently.

❹ Prepare a grill or preheat the broiler. If using a charcoal grill, see page 11 for instructions. Place patties on a vegetable grid. If broiling, place them on a broiler pan or large cookie sheet lined with a lightly oiled piece of aluminum foil. Grill or broil 3 to 5 inches from the heat, 5 to 7 minutes per side or until lightly browned. (When each side is done, turn the patties carefully with a spatula.) Check often to prevent burning.

➢ *Note:* For a more pronounced garlic flavor, don't sauté the garlic in Step 2. Add it raw to the kasha-mushroom mixture in Step 3 along with bread crumbs.

➢ *Serving Suggestions:* Serve on toasted onion rolls (or other bread of your choice) with chopped arugula, cucumber slices, maple mustard, and wine-glazed mushrooms. Garnish with carrot curls for a festive touch. These burgers also make a fine main course drizzled with Date-Raisin Chutney (page 121) and accompanied by a baked potatoe, steamed broccoli, and apple slices.

FALAFEL BURGERS

enjoy falafel, but have in the past often avoided it because it is deep-fried. Here is a burger prepared in the manner of falafel, but cooked by grilling or broiling rather than deep-frying.

Makes 7 to 8 patties, 3 to 4 servings

1 tablespoon olive oil
1 cup diced onion
1 tablespoon minced garlic
1 jalapeño pepper or other green
  chile of choice, cored, seeded,
  and minced (or to taste)
1½ cups cooked or
  1 (15-ounce) can
  chick-peas, drained
  (measured after draining)
1 cup cooked white basmati
  rice or other long-grain
  white rice
1 tablespoon freshly squeezed
  lime juice
1¾ cups Bread Crumbs
  (page 7) or commercial
  bread crumbs

Salt and freshly ground
  black pepper
Ground pasilla or red
  (or cayenne) pepper
  to taste

CONDIMENT SUGGESTIONS
(Choose from one or more
  of the following):
Red leaf lettuce, shredded
Vine-ripened tomato slices
Sweet onion slices
Alfalfa sprouts
Cucumber-Basil Raita
  (page 124)
Tahini Mustard (page 110)

GARNISH (OPTIONAL)
Lime wedges

❶ Heat the olive oil in a small skillet until sizzling. Cook the onion and garlic until the onion is wilted and the garlic is golden. Add the jalapeño and stir several times. Remove from heat and allow to cool.

❷ Place the onion mixture, drained chick-peas, and rice in the container of a food processor. Pulse on and off several times until the mixture becomes a smooth puree. Transfer to a large bowl. Add the lime juice and 1 cup of the bread crumbs. Season to taste with salt, black pepper, and red pepper. Mix with a large spoon or, even better, with your hands, until all ingredients are thoroughly combined.

❸ Shape into 3-inch patties ½ inch thick, adding extra bread crumbs if the patties don't hold their shape. They will be slightly sticky.

❹ Prepare a grill or preheat the broiler. If using a charcoal grill, see page 11 for instructions. Place the patties on a vegetable grid. If broiling, place the patties on a broiler pan or large cookie sheet lined with a lightly oiled piece of aluminum foil. Grill or broil 3 to 5 inches from the heat, 4 to 7 minutes per side or until lightly browned. (When one side is done, turn the patties carefully with a spatula.) Check often to prevent burning.

➤ *Serving Suggestions:* Tuck these falafels into warmed pita pockets along with shredded lettuce, tomato slices, onion slices, alfalfa sprouts, and a dollop of cucumber-basil raita and/or tahini mustard. Garnish with lime wedges. A glass of minted iced tea is just right with this meal. Alternatively, serve the patties as an entrée with Saffron Rice Pilaf (page 102) and a salad of radicchio, watercress, and toasted walnuts. Zippy Buttermilk Soup (page 100) makes an excellent starter course.

CURRIED KIDNEY
BEAN BURGERS

*I*ndian cooks appreciate kidney beans because of their robust, earthy flavor that stands up well to assertive spicing. The same Indian inspiration is at work here, but instead of the array of individual spices that an Indian cook works with, I use the more familiar commercial curry powder for convenience. The judicious use of fresh green chiles gives these burgers an even livelier flavor.

Makes 9 to 10 burgers, 4 to 5 servings

1 tablespoon canola oil
1 cup diced onion
1 tablespoon minced garlic
1 teaspoon curry powder
1 medium green bell pepper, cored, seeded, and coarsely chopped
2 tablespoons bean liquid (from kidney beans) or water
¾ cup cooked oatmeal (regular or instant)
1½ cups cooked or canned kidney beans, drained, cooking or can liquid retained (beans measured after draining)
1 large egg or 2 egg whites (optional)

1 jalapeño pepper or other green chile of choice, cored, seeded, and minced (or to taste)
1¾ cups Bread Crumbs (page 7) or commercial bread crumbs
Salt
Dash ground red (or cayenne) pepper

CONDIMENT SUGGESTIONS
(Choose from one or more of the following):
Jalapeño peppers, seeded, cut into thin rounds
Sweet onion, cut into paper-thin slices
Two-Cheese Spread (page 116)

❶ Heat the canola oil in a medium skillet over moderate heat. Cook the onion and garlic until the onion is wilted, about 2 minutes. Add the curry powder, bell pepper, and bean liquid. Bring to a boil. Reduce heat and simmer, covered, until the peppers are slightly softened, 3 to 4 minutes.

❷ Pour the contents of the skillet along with the oatmeal, beans, and the optional egg or egg whites into the container of a food processor. Pulse on and off several times until the ingredients are thoroughly blended. Transfer to a large bowl and add the jalapeño and 1 cup of the bread crumbs. Season to taste with salt and red pepper. Mix with your hands until all ingredients are thoroughly combined.

❸ Shape into patties 3 inches in diameter and ½ inch thick, adding extra bread crumbs if the patties don't hold their shape. They will be delicate, so handle them gently.

❹ Prepare a grill or preheat the broiler. If using a charcoal grill, see page 11 for instructions. Place the patties on a vegetable grid. If broiling, place the patties on a broiler pan or large cookie sheet lined with a lightly oiled piece of aluminum foil. Grill or broil 3 to 5 inches from the heat, 6 to 8 minutes per side or until lightly browned. Check often to prevent burning.

➤ *Serving Suggestions:* Shape the patties like sausages and serve wrapped in warm tortillas (or put on other bread of your choice) with jalapeño rounds, sweet onion slices, and two-cheese spread. Try carrot, green bell pepper, and celery sticks on the side. Or, serve the patties as an entrée with orzo cooked in vegetable broth, steamed squash, and a spinach-walnut salad. A cool, refreshing plate of ripe papaya slices or other seasonal fresh fruit will bring the meal to a fine conclusion.

QUINOA AND BLACK BEAN BURGERS

*h*ere dense, deeply flavorful black beans team up with light, fluffy quinoa and a mélange of Indian and Western seasonings. The result is a burger that is hearty yet not heavy, bursting with the rich taste of a North Indian kebab.

Makes 10 to 11 burgers, 3 to 4 servings

½ cup quinoa, rinsed
several times
1 tablespoon canola oil
1 cup diced onion
1 tablespoon minced garlic
¼ teaspoon ground turmeric
1 teaspoon ground cumin
1 tablespoon ground cinnamon
1 red or green bell pepper,
cored, seeded, and
coarsely chopped
2 tablespoons ketchup
Several dashes Worcestershire
sauce
1½ cups cooked or canned
black beans, drained
(measured after draining)

6 pecans, toasted and finely
chopped, plus ¼ cup pecans,
toasted and ground in
a spice/coffee grinder to a
coarse powder
2 cups Bread Crumbs
(page 7) or commercial
bread crumbs
Salt and freshly ground
black pepper
CONDIMENT SUGGESTIONS
(Choose from one or more
of the following):
Shredded romaine lettuce
Sour cream (regular or nonfat)
Hoisin sauce
GARNISH (OPTIONAL)
Cherry tomatoes

❶ Place the quinoa and 1 cup water in a medium-sized saucepan and bring to a boil. Reduce heat and simmer, covered, until all water is absorbed and quinoa is light and fluffy, 15 to 20 minutes. Measure 1 cup and set aside. (Retain the excess for later use.)
❷ Heat the canola oil in a medium-sized skillet over moderate heat. Cook the onion and garlic until the onion is wilted. Add turmeric, cumin, and cinnamon and stir until they are well

distributed. Add the bell pepper, ketchup, and Worcestershire sauce. Cook, covered, until the bell pepper turns pale and softens, 7 to 10 minutes. During this period, uncover once or twice and stir, adding a teaspoon of water if the mixture is beginning to stick to the bottom of the skillet.

❸ Place the onion mixture, the reserved 1 cup quinoa, and drained black beans in the container of a food processor. Process until the ingredients are thoroughly blended. Transfer to a large bowl. Add the chopped and ground pecans and 1¼ cups of the bread crumbs. Season to taste with salt and pepper. Mix with your hands until all ingredients are thoroughly combined. Shape into patties 3 inches in diameter and ½ inch thick, mixing in extra bread crumbs if the patties don't hold their shape.

❹ Prepare a grill or preheat the broiler. If using a charcoal grill, see page 11 for instructions. Place the patties on a vegetable grid. If broiling, place the patties on a broiler pan or large cookie sheet lined with a lightly oiled piece of aluminum foil. Grill or broil 3 to 5 inches from the heat, 6 to 9 minutes per side or until lightly browned. Check often to prevent burning.

➤ *Serving Suggestions:* Place on a bed of shredded romaine (or put on toasted buns of choice) and top each serving with a dollop each of sour cream and hoisin sauce. Garnish the plate with cherry tomatoes if you like. A side dish of fresh pineapple slices makes a delightful accompaniment. Or, serve the patties as an entrée with quinoa on the side. Black beans have an affinity with carrots, so either carrot soup or candied carrots will do nicely as a side dish.

➤ **VEGETARIAN HOT "BEEF" SANDWICH:** For a special treat, place the burgers, open-faced, on toasted bun of your choice. Spoon heated Mushroom "Cream" Sauce (page 117) over them. (You can serve any burger recipe in this book this way.)

REFRIED BEAN BURGERS WITH CHIPOTLE PEPPER

1his recipe, a blend of refried beans and rice, accented with hauntingly smoky, fiery chipotle peppers, owes its inspiration to the traditional bean cookery of Mexico. The wild rice imparts a delightfully chewy taste.

Makes 8 to 9 burgers, 4 servings

1 tablespoon canola oil
1 cup diced onion
1 tablespoon minced garlic
1 large bell pepper (preferably red or golden), cored, seeded, and diced
1 tablespoon ground cumin
1 cup cooked brown basmati rice, preferably (or other long-grain brown rice)
¼ cup cooked wild rice
1¾ cups cooked and mashed pinto beans, or 1 (16-ounce) can vegetarian refried beans

2 cups Bread Crumbs (page 7) or commercial bread crumbs
Dash ground chipotle pepper (to taste; see Note)
Salt

CONDIMENT SUGGESTIONS
(Choose one or both of the following):
Shredded Bibb lettuce
Salsa International (page 123)

❶ Heat the canola oil in a medium skillet over moderate heat. Add the onion and garlic and cook until the onion is wilted. Add the bell pepper and cumin. Reduce heat and cook, covered, until the bell pepper is tender, 5 to 10 minutes. (The vegetables will cook in their own liquid.) During this period, uncover, and stir in a little water (up to 2 teaspoons) if the mixture sticks to the bottom.

❷ Place the onion-bell pepper mixture, brown rice, wild rice, and refried beans in a food processor and process until smooth. (Some of the wild rice will not break down. This is to be expected. It will contribute to the final texture.) Transfer to a large bowl. Add 1½ cups of the bread crumbs and season to taste with chipotle pepper and salt. Mix with your hands until all ingredients are thoroughly combined. Form into patties 3 inches in diameter and ½ inch thick, mixing in extra bread crumbs if the patties don't hold their shape.

❸ Prepare a grill or preheat the broiler. If using a charcoal grill, see page 11 for instructions. Place the patties on a vegetable grid. If broiling, place the patties on a broiler pan or large cookie sheet lined with a lightly oiled piece of aluminum foil. Grill or broil 3 to 5 inches from the heat, 5 to 7 minutes per side or until lightly browned. Check often to prevent burning.

❹ Manual method: These burgers can be prepared without a food processor. In this case, mince the onion and bell pepper. Proceed with the instructions through Step 1. Then place all the ingredients except the bread crumbs and salt in a large bowl. Mix well, using a spoon or your hands. Now add bread crumbs, season to taste with salt, and prepare patties as in Step 2.

➤ *Note:* Use either ground chipotle pepper or canned chipotle chile, preserved in sauce. In either case, start with a small amount, as chipotle chile is quite hot. Add a little at a time until the desired taste is achieved.

➤ *Serving Suggestions:* Place on toasted Italian peasant bread (or other bread of your choice) with Bibb lettuce and salsa international. Or serve burrito-style in a warm whole wheat tortilla with shredded lettuce, chopped onion, and salsa international or your favorite salsa. In this case, cut the burgers in halves and place end to end in the tortilla. These patties also make a substantial main course when accompanied by couscous and Ginger and Wine-sauced Green Beans (page 95).

RED LENTIL AND MILLET BURGERS

f all the varieties of lentils that can be used to prepare vegetarian burgers, my favorite, by far, is the red lentil. It cooks the quickest, blends smoothly with grains and vegetables, and takes well to a host of spices. Here, red lentils are combined with millet, carrots, and scallions to produce a burger that will satisfy the heartiest of appetites.

Makes 11 burgers, 5 servings

½ cup red lentils
½ cup millet
1 tablespoon canola oil, plus
  additional for sautéing
  (optional)
2 cups finely chopped scallions
½ pound grated carrots
  (about 1¾ cups)
1 tablespoon vegetarian oyster
  sauce (if unavailable,
  substitute hoisin sauce)
1 tablespoon ketchup
¼ cup sesame seeds, toasted
  and ground to a coarse

powder in a spice/coffee
  grinder or with mortar
  and pestle
1¾ cups Bread Crumbs
  (page 7) or commercial
  bread crumbs
Salt

CONDIMENT SUGGESTIONS
(Choose from one or both
  of the following):
Radicchio leaves
Plum Chutney (page 122)

GARNISH (OPTIONAL)
Cilantro sprigs

❶ Bring the red lentils and 1¼ cups water to a boil. Reduce heat and simmer, covered, until the lentils are tender, 10 to 15 minutes. (Their color will turn pale and they will break easily when pressed between two fingers.) Remove from heat. With a slotted spoon remove the lentils from the pan, pressing out as much water as possible. Measure 1 cup and set aside. (Retain the excess for later use.)

❷ Bring the millet and 1 cup water to a boil in a separate pan. Reduce heat and simmer, covered, until all water is absorbed and millet is tender, 10 to 15 minutes. Measure 1 cup and reserve. (Retain the excess for later use.)

❸ Heat the canola oil in a large skillet over moderate heat. Add the scallions and cook for a few minutes or until they are wilted. Add the carrots, vegetarian oyster sauce, and ketchup. Cook, uncovered, for about 5 minutes to blend the flavors, stirring often.

❹ Place the reserved red lentils, millet, and the carrot-scallion mixture in a food processor. Process until a smooth and fine-textured purée results. Transfer to a large bowl. Add the ground sesame seeds and 1 cup of the bread crumbs. Season to taste with salt. Mix with a large spoon or, even better, with your hands, until all ingredients are thoroughly combined. Form into patties 3-inches in diameter and ½ inch thick, mixing in extra bread crumbs if the patties don't hold their shape. They will be delicate, but easy to work with.

❺ Prepare a grill or preheat the broiler. If using a charcoal grill, see page 11 for instructions. Place the patties on a vegetable grid. If broiling, place the patties on a broiler pan or large cookie sheet lined with a lightly oiled piece of aluminum foil. Grill or broil 3 to 5 inches from the heat, 5 to 7 minutes per side or until lightly browned. (Turn the patties carefully with a spatula when one side is done.) Check often to prevent burning.

➤ *Sautéing method:* Instead of grilling or broiling, you can sauté these burgers. Heat 1 tablespoon canola oil in a medium skillet over moderate heat until sizzling. Cook 2 to 3 patties at a time over medium heat until medium brown at the bottom, a few minutes. Turn the patties and cook the other side the same way, adjusting heat to prevent burning. Repeat the process for the rest of the patties, adding extra oil as necessary to prevent sticking.

➤ *Serving Suggestions:* Serve on toasted French country bread (or other bread of your choice), layered with radicchio and drizzled with plum chutney. (For extra protein, spread ricotta or cottage cheese on top of burgers.) Garnish with cilantro sprigs. Or, serve the patties as an entrée with brown basmati rice and Three-Pepper Sauté (page 87). Follow with some Asian pear or Bosc pear slices.

VEGETABLE BURGERS

BEET AND MUSHROOM BURGERS 34

PEA BURGERS 36

GREEN BURGERS 38

TRIPLE MUSHROOM BURGERS 40

*t*here is a strong emphasis on fresh vegetables in these burgers, a sort of farmers' market on a plate. Although most vegetables can be used, the recipes specify those I have found particularly useful. Since the vegetables are cooked and puréed first, their size or shape is less important than their taste and texture. Potatoes, for instance, provide body and help a burger hold its shape; mushrooms impart a texture and taste reminiscent of meat; and carrots add a nuance of sweetness to the final product. Leafy greens such as Swiss chard, beet greens, or spinach, in combination with other vegetables, also produce savory patties.

Here, with the exception of potatoes, vegetables alone will yield a mushy burger that may not hold its shape. So grains, nuts, and seeds, which have the ability to bind other ingredients together, are used. The end result is a substantial, texturally pleasant eating experience, akin to the traditional meat-based burger. Rice, bulgur, and bread crumbs are the common grains and grain derivatives that appear most frequently in these recipes. All work equally well prepared either fresh or as leftovers. Almonds, sesame seeds, and sunflower seeds not only enhance the texture of these burgers but also impart a rich, nutty quality to the overall taste.

Many of these vegetarian patties contain reduced amounts of grains, so they tend to be lighter and a bit more fragile. They are ideal for lunch or, paired with a bean dish of your choice and, perhaps, a salad, at a main meal. Alternatively, accompany them with a hearty bean stew, Indian-style, or serve them with a robust vegetable soup.

BEET AND MUSHROOM BURGERS

*t*ender and moist, these deep, reddish purple patties look especially attractive on a grill and are perfect for a summer barbecue.

Makes 8 burgers, 4 servings

¾ pound beets, scraped to removed root hairs, if any, cut into 1-inch cubes (scant 3 cups; see Note)
1 tablespoon olive oil
1 cup diced onion
1 tablespoon minced garlic
1 jalapeño pepper or other green chile of choice, cored, seeded, and chopped (or to taste)
¼ pound fresh mushrooms, sliced ¼ inch thick
1 cup cooked white basmati rice or other long-grain white rice
2 tablespoons ketchup
¼ cup shelled, raw sunflower seeds, toasted and ground to

a coarse powder in a blender or food processor
1¾ cups Bread Crumbs (page 7) or commercial bread crumbs
Salt

CONDIMENT SUGGESTIONS
(Choose from one or more of the following):
Chopped scallions
Steamed pea pods (plain or brushed with dark sesame oil)
Whole shiso (or basil or mint) leaves
Honey-Ginger Mustard (page 111)

❶ Steam the beets until tender, 18 to 25 minutes.
❷ Heat the olive oil in a medium skillet over moderate heat. Add the onion and garlic and cook until the onion is wilted. Add the jalapeño and mushrooms. Reduce heat and cook, covered, for 4 to 5 minutes or just until the mushrooms are tender. With a slotted spoon, remove the vegetables and place them in a medium bowl. Cook the liquid remaining in the skillet, if any, over

medium heat until it is quite thick, a few minutes. Pour this sauce over the onion-mushroom mixture.

❸ Place steamed beets, the onion-mushroom mixture, rice, and ketchup in a food processor. Pulse on and off several times until the ingredients are thoroughly blended. Transfer to a large bowl. Add ground sunflower seeds and 1 cup of the bread crumbs and season to taste with salt. Mix with a large spoon or, even better, with your hands, until all ingredients are thoroughly combined. Form into patties 3 inches in diameter and ½ inch thick, mixing in extra bread crumbs if the patties don't hold their shape. They will be delicate, so handle them gently.

❹ Prepare a grill or preheat the broiler. If using a charcoal grill, see page 11 for instructions. Place the patties on a vegetable grid. If broiling, place the patties on a broiler pan or large cookie sheet lined with a lightly oiled piece of aluminum foil. Grill or broil 3 to 5 inches from the heat. When the tops are lightly browned (approximately 5 to 7 minutes), turn carefully with a spatula and cook until the other side is browned. Check often to prevent burning.

➤ *Note:* You can keep the beets whole, which results in less "bleeding." In this case, adjust the steaming time in Step 1 and dice them into 1-inch cubes after they can be pierced easily with a fork.

➤ *Serving Suggestions:* Serve on warmed baguette with scallions, pea pods, shiso, basil or mint leaves, and honey-ginger mustard. As an entrée, these patties are a lively foil for couscous and Ginger and Wine-sauced Green Beans (page 95).

PEA BURGERS

hese burgers are a hearty combination of peas, rutabaga, and almonds, delicately seasoned with turmeric and garam masala. They are topped with a tender sauté of Asian greens such as baby bok choy or mizuna mustard greens, whose pleasantly bitter taste provides an ideal contrast to the sweetness of the peas.

Makes 8 burgers, 4 servings

½ pound rutabaga, scraped to remove root hairs if any, or potatoes, peeled and cubed, cut into 1-inch cubes (2 cups)

2 cups fresh peas or thawed frozen peas

1 tablespoon olive oil

1 cup diced onion

1 tablespoon minced garlic

1 jalapeño pepper or other green chile of choice, cored, seeded, and minced (or to taste)

¼ teaspoon ground turmeric

1 teaspoon garam masala

3 tablespoons chopped black (kalamata) olives

1 large egg or 2 egg whites (optional)

¼ cup slivered almonds, toasted and ground to a coarse powder in a spice/coffee grinder

2 cups Bread Crumbs (page 7) or commercial bread crumbs

Salt

CONDIMENT SUGGESTIONS (Choose from one or more of the following):

Sweet onion slices

Peeled cucumber slices

Basil "Mayonnaise" (page 116)

Wilted Baby Greens (page 96)

❶ Steam the rutabaga or potatoes until tender, 15 to 20 minutes. Mash thoroughly.
❷ If using fresh peas, steam until tender, 7 to 10 minutes. (Thawed frozen peas don't require steaming.)
❸ Heat the olive oil in a small skillet over moderate heat. Add the onion and garlic and cook until the onion is translucent. Add the jalapeño and turmeric and stir until evenly distributed.
❹ Place the mashed rutabaga, peas, onion-garlic mixture, garam masala, olives, and the optional egg or egg whites in the

container of a food processor. Process until the ingredients are blended. The mixture need not be very smooth. Scrape into a large bowl. Add the ground almonds and 1¼ cups of the bread crumbs. Season to taste with salt. Mix with your hands until all ingredients are thoroughly combined. Form into patties 3 inches in diameter and ½ inch thick, mixing in extra bread crumbs if the patties don't hold their shape.

❺ Prepare a grill or preheat the broiler. If using a charcoal grill, see page 11 for instructions. Place the patties on a vegetable grid. If broiling, place them on a broiler pan or large cookie sheet lined with a lightly oiled piece of aluminum foil dusted with bread crumbs. Grill or broil 3 to 5 inches from the heat, 6 to 9 minutes per side or until the tops look set and/or lightly browned. (When one side is done, turn patties carefully with a spatula.) Check often to prevent burning.

➤ *Serving Suggestions:* Serve on toasted black bread (or other bread of your choice) with onion, cucumber, and basil "mayonnaise." Mound wilted baby greens on top of the burgers or serve on the side. As an entrée, these patties complement baked potato with Two-Cheese Spread (page 116) and a platter of mixed, steamed vegetables, such as carrots, broccoli, and zucchini, dressed with Lime Vinaigrette (page 94).

GREEN BURGERS

combination of leafy greens and mushrooms give these burgers a unique, earthy taste. Bits of sun-dried tomatoes provide a bright sunny accent. Swiss chard is my choice of green here, but you can use any other hearty green such as mustard, kale, collard, or spinach. The seasoning, a blend of garlic, ginger, sesame oil, sesame seeds, and chile paste, is Korean-inspired.

Makes 8 burgers, 4 servings

½ pound Swiss chard, stemmed, and coarsely shredded (4 firmly packed cups; see Note)
1 tablespoon dark sesame oil
3 to 5 large garlic cloves, minced
1 tablespoon minced ginger root
¼ pound fresh mushrooms, sliced ¼ inch thick
¼ teaspoon sambal oelek (or to taste)
2 tablespoons sesame seeds, toasted and ground to a coarse powder in a spice/coffee grinder or with mortar and pestle
1 cup prepared Bulgur (page 8)

1 large egg or 2 egg whites (optional)
6 to 8 oil-cured sun-dried tomatoes, drained and minced
1½ cups Bread Crumbs (page 7) or commercial bread crumbs
Salt and freshly ground black pepper

CONDIMENT SUGGESTIONS
(Choose from one or more of the following):
Sesame Eggplant Steaks (page 104)
Raw, sweet onion rings
Alfalfa sprouts
Chopped scallions

GARNISH (OPTIONAL)
Scallion curls

❶ Steam the chard until tender, 5 to 8 minutes. Allow to cool to room temperature.

❷ Heat the sesame oil in a large skillet over moderate heat. Sauté the garlic and ginger until the garlic is golden. Add the mushrooms and sambal oelek. Cook, uncovered, until the

mushrooms soften, 4 to 6 minutes, stirring often. Add the ground sesame seeds and mix well. Remove from heat and allow to cool.
❸ Place the chard, garlic-mushroom mixture, softened bulgur, and the optional egg or egg whites in a food processor. Pulse on and off several times until the ingredients are thoroughly blended. Transfer to a large bowl. Add the minced sun-dried tomatoes and 1 cup of the bread crumbs; season to taste with salt and pepper. Mix with a large spoon or, even better, with your hands, until all ingredients are thoroughly combined. Form into patties 3 inches in diameter and ½ inch thick. Mix in more bread crumbs if the patties don't hold their shape. The patties will be delicate, so handle them gently.
❹ Prepare a grill or preheat the broiler. If using a charcoal grill, see page 11 for instructions. Place the patties on a vegetable grid. If broiling, place the patties on a broiler pan or large cookie sheet lined with a lightly oiled piece of aluminum foil. Grill or broil 3 to 5 inches from the heat, 7 to 9 minutes per side or until lightly browned. (When one side is done, turn patties carefully with a spatula.) Check often to prevent burning.
➤ *Note:* If using other greens, adjust steaming time according to their texture. Spinach (thoroughly rinsed) or beet greens, for example, are quite tender and will only need to be steamed 3 to 5 minutes. Less delicate greens such as collard or kale will require approximately 8 to 10 minutes.
➤ *Serving Suggestions:* Serve on toasted onion rolls (or other bread of your choice) with sesame eggplant steaks, onion rings, alfalfa sprouts, and scallions. Garnish each plate with scallion curls if you like. At the table, pass soy sauce, sesame oil, and sambal oelek to be mixed together and used as a condiment. As an entrée these patties are excellent with quinoa, Gingery Tomato Soup with Tofu (page 98) and Beet Salad with Lime and Pine Nuts (page 93). A plate of orange segments provides a fitting end to a colorful meal.

TRIPLE MUSHROOM BURGERS

hese burgers are a celebration of the diversity of mushrooms, shiitake, chanterelles, and portobello being among the popular varieties. The standard supermarket cultivated mushrooms will also do, alone or in combination with other more exotic types. To enhance the complex musky flavor of these burgers, hoisin sauce is added to the liquid left after cooking mushrooms.

Makes 12 burgers, 6 servings

1 tablespoon canola oil
1 cup diced onion
1 tablespoon minced garlic
1 jalapeño pepper or other green chile of choice, cored, seeded, and chopped (or to taste)
1 red bell pepper, cored, seeded, and coarsely chopped
1 pound fresh mushrooms (a mixture of shiitake, chanterelle, portobello, or others and/or the standard supermarket cultivated variety), sliced ¼ to ½ inch thick, tough stems removed if necessary
2 tablespoons hoisin sauce

1 cup cooked white basmati rice, preferably (or other long-grain white rice)
¼ cup pecans, toasted and ground to a coarse powder in a spice/coffee grinder
1½ cups Bread Crumbs (page 7) or commercial bread crumbs
Salt

CONDIMENT SUGGESTIONS
(Choose from one or more of the following):
Watercress or shredded romaine lettuce
Raw, sweet onion rings
Chipotle Ketchup (page 120)

❶ Heat the canola oil in a large skillet over moderate heat. Cook the onion and garlic until the onion turns brown at the edges and the garlic is golden. Add the jalapeño, bell pepper, and mushrooms. Reduce heat. Cover and cook until the vegetables are tender, 10 to 15 minutes. (The vegetables will cook in their own liquid. Uncover occasionally and check to see if the mixture is sticking. If so, stir in up to a tablespoon of water.) Add the hoisin sauce and mix well. With a slotted spoon, remove the vegetables and place them in a large bowl.

❷ Reduce sauce remaining in the skillet by placing over medium heat. Cook, uncovered, stirring often, until the sauce is very thick, 5 to 10 minutes. Pour sauce over the onion–mushroom mixture.

❸ Place the onion–mushroom mixture and the rice in a food processor. Pulse on and off several times until the ingredients are thoroughly blended. Transfer to a large bowl and add the ground pecans and 1¼ cups of the bread crumbs. Season to taste with salt. Mix with a large spoon or, even better, with your hands, until all ingredients are thoroughly combined. Form into patties 3 inches in diameter and ½ inch thick, mixing in extra bread crumbs if the patties don't hold their shape. They will be delicate, so handle them gently.

❹ Prepare a grill or preheat the broiler. If using a charcoal grill, see page 11 for instructions. Place the patties on a vegetable grid. If broiling, place the patties on a broiler pan or large cookie sheet lined with a lightly oiled piece of aluminum foil. Grill or broil 3 to 5 inches from the heat, 5 to 7 minutes per side or until lightly browned. (When one side is done, turn the patties to the other side with a spatula.) Check often to prevent burning.

➤ *Serving Suggestions:* These burgers are best served on toasted garlic rolls (or other bread of your choice) with watercress, onion, and chipotle ketchup. Or, serve as a main course with kasha, a crisp coleslaw, and extra hoisin sauce. Finish the meal with fresh peach or pear slices.

NUT AND SEED BURGERS

CASHEW BURGERS   46

PEANUT BURGERS   48

PECAN MUSHROOM BURGERS   50

ZUCCHINI BURGERS WITH PINE NUTS AND
SUN-DRIED TOMATOES   52

WINTER SQUASH AND PUMPKIN
SEED BURGERS   54

Crushed nuts and seeds combined with vegetables and grains produce sumptuous burgers. I take my inspiration for them from the ancient cultures of India, the Middle East, and Mexico, where nuts and seeds have been used to enrich and thicken sauces for millennia. During burger preparation, ground nuts and seeds absorb moisture, help the patties hold their shape, and improve texture, flavor, and nutritional content. Almonds, cashews, pumpkin seeds, and sesame seeds each add a unique taste.

I like to start with whole or halved nuts, rather than nut butters, which are quite expensive and not as readily available. One exception is the ubiquitous and inexpensive peanut butter. It is also easier to work with than whole peanuts and blends easily with other ingredients.

Seeds work equally well. Sunflower seeds are better known, but pumpkin seeds have a richer, more complex flavor that combines perfectly with such varied ingredients as tofu or winter squash. And sesame seeds, ground to a fine powder, contribute a buttery quality to burgers.

Lightly toasting nuts and seeds before grinding or chopping helps intensify their flavor. I add them in two stages: ground nuts as a main ingredient; a lesser amount of chopped nuts for textural contrast and concentrated nuggets of roasted nut flavor.

Used to excess, nuts and seeds can add unnecessarily to the fat content of a burger. In judicious amounts, however, they have no equal as flavor and texture enhancers.

CASHEW BURGERS

ich, roasted cashews and nutrient-dense broccoli are combined to create these superb-tasting burgers. A wealth of other vegetables — potatoes, carrots, and mushrooms among them — are found in the supporting cast.

Makes 12 burgers, 6 servings

½ pound potatoes, peeled and cut into 1-inch cubes (scant 2 cups)

¼ pound carrots, diced (about 1 cup)

¼ pound broccoli florets, cut into small pieces (about 2 cups)

1 tablespoon olive oil

1 cup diced onion

2 teaspoons minced ginger root

1 tablespoon minced garlic

¼ pound fresh mushrooms, sliced ¼ inch thick

1 red bell pepper, cored, seeded, and coarsely chopped

2 tablespoons ketchup

½ teaspoon tamari

¾ teaspoon sambal oelek or red chili paste (or to taste)

1 cup prepared Bulgur (page 8)

¾ cup unsalted raw cashew pieces, ground in a spice/coffee grinder to a coarse powder

1¾ cups Bread Crumbs (page 7) or commercial bread crumbs

Salt

CONDIMENT SUGGESTIONS (Choose from one or more of the following):

Chopped arugula and/or young mizuna mustard greens

Radish slices

Peeled cucumber slices

Apricot Mustard (page 110) or Maple Mustard (page 111)

GARNISH (OPTIONAL)

Orange segments

❶ Steam the potatoes and carrots until both are tender, 15 to 20 minutes. Steam the broccoli separately for 7 to 10 minutes or until tender. (Alternatively, you can add the broccoli to the potatoes and carrots during the last 7 to 10 minutes of steaming.) Set aside.
❷ Heat the olive oil in a large skillet over moderate heat. Add the

onion and cook until it is wilted, about 2 minutes. Add the ginger and garlic and stir to distribute them evenly. Add the mushrooms, bell pepper, ketchup, tamari, and sambal oelek. Reduce heat and cook, covered, until the vegetables are tender, 6 to 10 minutes. (The vegetables will cook in their own liquid. Uncover occasionally and stir in a teaspoon or two of water if the mixture is sticking to the bottom of the skillet.) With a slotted spoon, remove the vegetables to a large bowl. If any sauce has accumulated at the bottom, reduce it over medium heat to a syrupy consistency, stirring often. Pour sauce over the vegetables.

❸ In a food processor, place steamed potatoes, carrots, broccoli, onion-mushroom mixture, and bulgur. Pulse on and off several times until thoroughly blended. Transfer to a large bowl and add ground cashews and 1¼ cups of the bread crumbs. Mix with a large spoon or, even better, with your hands, until all ingredients are thoroughly combined. Season to taste with salt. Form into 12 patties, each 3 inches in diameter and ½ inch thick. The mixture will be very soft and sticky. Mix in extra bread crumbs if the patties don't hold their shape. They will firm up during cooking.

❹ Prepare a grill or preheat the broiler. If using a charcoal grill, see page 11 for instructions. Place the patties on a vegetable grid. If broiling, place the patties on a broiler pan or large cookie sheet lined with a lightly oiled piece of aluminum foil. Grill or broil 3 to 5 inches from the heat, 6 to 7 minutes per side or until lightly browned. (When one side is done, turn patties carefully with a spatula.) Check often to prevent burning.

➤ *Serving Suggestions:* Serve on your favorite rolls with arugula, radish slices, cucumber, and apricot or maple mustard. Garnish the plates with orange segments. These patties are excellent as a main course accompanied by Saffron Rice Pilaf (page 102), Wilted Baby Greens (page 96), and Date-Raisin Chutney (page 121).

PEANUT BURGERS

*he principal seasoning here is South Indian sambhar powder,
a ground mixture of cumin, fenugreek, and curry leaves. This
bold spice mix blends well with mushrooms, bell pepper, and peanut
butter to create these burgers. Their sensuous flavor is further
enhanced with peanut sauce, reminiscent of that which is served
throughout Southeast Asia.*

Makes 8 burgers, 4 servings

1 tablespoon canola oil
1 cup diced onion
1 tablespoon coarsely
  chopped ginger root
1 large red or golden yellow
  bell pepper, cored, seeded,
  and coarsely chopped
½ pound fresh mushrooms,
  sliced ¼ inch thick
1½ to 2 teaspoons
  sambhar powder
1 cup cooked oatmeal (regular
  or instant) or cooked millet
½ cup crunchy peanut butter

1 large egg or 2 egg whites
  (optional)
2 cups Bread Crumbs
  (page 7) or commercial
  bread crumbs
Salt and freshly ground
  black pepper
CONDIMENT SUGGESTIONS
(Choose from one or more
  of the following):
Sweet onion slices
Fresh Herb Plate (page 126)
Peanut Sauce (page 112)

❶ Heat the canola oil in a large skillet over moderate heat. Cook
the onion and ginger root until the onion is wilted. Add the bell
pepper, mushrooms, and sambhar powder. Reduce heat. Cover and
cook just until the vegetables are tender, 6 to 10 minutes. With a
slotted spoon, remove the vegetables and place them in a large
bowl. If any liquid remains in the skillet, reduce over medium heat
to a syrupy consistency, 2 to 5 minutes, stirring often.
❷ Place the bell pepper–mushroom mixture, the thickened sauce,
oatmeal, peanut butter, and the optional egg or egg whites in a
food processor. Pulse on and off several times until the mixture
is thoroughly blended. Transfer to a large bowl and add 1¼ cups

of the bread crumbs. Mix with a large spoon or, even better, with your hands, until all ingredients are thoroughly combined. Season to taste with salt and black pepper. Form into 8 patties ½ inch thick and 3 inches in diameter, mixing in extra bread crumbs if the patties don't hold their shape.

❸ Prepare a grill or preheat the broiler. If using a charcoal grill, see page 11 for instructions. Place the patties on a vegetable grid. If broiling, place the patties on a broiler pan or large cookie sheet lined with a lightly oiled piece of aluminum foil dusted with bread crumbs. Grill or broil 3 to 5 inches from the heat, 5 to 7 minutes per side or until lightly browned. (When one side is done, turn patties carefully with a spatula.) Check often to prevent burning.

➤ *Serving Suggestions:* Enjoy on toasted English muffins with onion, herbs, and peanut sauce. Alternatively, serve the patties as a main course with quinoa and a spinach-mushroom salad. Kiwi slices and orange segments would be a nice way to finish the meal.

➤ **PEANUT LOAF:** This savory vegetarian loaf is an ideal entrée anytime during the year, but particularly in autumn and winter. Preheat the oven to 400 degrees. Prepare the mixture and process as in Step 2 above, except increase the number of whole eggs to 3 large, or use 6 egg whites. Instead of forming into patties, put the mixture in a standard loaf pan (such as an 8½ x 4½ x 3-inch size) that has been lightly oiled or sprayed with cooking spray. Bake for 15 to 20 minutes or just until the top turns medium brown and the center feels firm when lightly pressed with the finger. Allow to cool slightly. Serve with Indian Ketchup (page 119) and Maple Mustard (page 111).

For best results, make the loaf a day ahead and refrigerate. The flavors will blend and the loaf will be easier to slice. Reheat in a 325-degree oven for 8 to 15 minutes before serving.

Serve any leftovers sandwich-style with your favorite burger trimmings.

PECAN MUSHROOM BURGERS

a subtle, earthy mushroom flavor permeates these burgers in which you will also experience the crunchiness of pecans and the chewy texture of bulgur. Two good choices for mushroom are portobello, which has a haunting woodsy flavor, or fresh shiitake, with its fine, meaty texture. In a pinch, try using standard supermarket mushrooms or dried mushrooms that have been reconstituted by soaking in hot water. The aromatic garlic purée that is spread on the bread is an added bonus.

Makes 10 burgers, 5 servings

1 tablespoon olive oil
3 to 5 large garlic
  cloves, minced
1 cup coarsely chopped
  scallions
½ pound fresh portobello,
  shiitake, or other mushroom
  of choice, tough stems
  removed if necessary, sliced
  ¼ to ½ inch thick
¼ pound Swiss chard leaves,
  stems removed and coarsely
  chopped (2 firmly
  packed cups)
2 teaspoons tamari
1 teaspoon rice vinegar

1 cup prepared Bulgur
  (page 8)
¼ cup pecans, toasted and
  ground to a coarse powder
  in a spice/coffee grinder
1¾ cups Bread Crumbs
  (page 7) or commercial
  bread crumbs
Salt and freshly ground
  black pepper

CONDIMENT SUGGESTIONS
(Choose from one or more
  of the following):
Shredded cabbage
Raw, sweet onion rings
Roasted Garlic Purée (page 114)

❶ Heat the oil in a medium-sized skillet over moderate heat. Cook the garlic until it is golden. Stir in the scallions. Add the mushrooms, chard, tamari, and rice vinegar. Cook, covered, until the vegetables are softened, 6 to 8 minutes. (If overcooked, chard will lose its color.) With a slotted spoon, remove the vegetables and place them in a large bowl. Cook the liquid that has accumulated in the bottom of the skillet over medium heat, stirring often. In a few minutes, when it thickens to a syrupy consistency, pour it over the vegetables.

❷ Place the garlic-mushroom mixture and the bulgur in the container of a food processor. Pulse on and off several times until the mixture is thoroughly blended. Scrape into a large bowl; add the ground pecans and 1 cup of the bread crumbs. Mix with a large spoon or, even better, with your hands, until all ingredients are thoroughly combined. Season to taste with salt and black pepper. Form into patties ½ inch thick and 3 inches in diameter, mixing in extra bread crumbs if the patties don't hold their shape.

❸ Prepare a grill or preheat the broiler. If using a charcoal grill, see page 11 for instructions. Place the patties on a vegetable grid. If broiling, place the patties on a broiler pan or large cookie sheet lined with a lightly oiled piece of aluminum foil. Grill or broil 3 to 5 inches from the heat, 7 to 9 minutes per side or until lightly browned. (When one side is done, turn the patties carefully with a spatula.) Check often to prevent burning.

➢ *Serving Suggestions:* Enjoy on focaccia bread with shredded cabbage, sweet onion rings, and roasted garlic purée. The patties are also great served as an entrée with Double-Garlic Potatoes (page 92) and red bell pepper slices.

➢ **SHISO VARIATION:** Strongly flavored Japanese shiso leaves have an affinity for mushrooms and enhance the taste of these burgers. Add 2 tablespoons minced shiso leaves to the processed mixture in Step 2.

ZUCCHINI BURGERS WITH PINE NUTS AND SUN-DRIED TOMATOES

his is a burger with a sunny Mediterranean accent. Good by itself, it's even more inviting when topped with a well-spiced Indian-inspired ketchup.

Makes 11 to 12 burgers, 5 to 6 servings

2 tablespoons olive oil
1 cup diced onion
½ cup prepared Bulgur
(page 8)
1 teaspoon sugar
1 tablespoon minced garlic
2 cups shredded zucchini
¼ cup minced fresh basil leaves
5 to 6 oil-cured sun-dried
tomatoes, drained
and minced
½ cup pine nuts, toasted and
ground to a coarse powder
in a spice/coffee grinder
2 cups Bread Crumbs
(page 7) or commercial
bread crumbs

Salt and freshly ground
black pepper
CONDIMENT SUGGESTIONS
(Choose from one or more
of the following):
Whole basil leaves (a mixture
of regular and purple basil,
if available)
Tomato slices
Indian Ketchup (page 119)
Wine-glazed Mushrooms
(page 101)

❶ Heat 1 tablespoon of the olive oil in a saucepan over moderate heat. Cook the onion until it is translucent. Add the bulgur, sugar, and 2 cups water. Cover and bring to a boil. Reduce heat and simmer, covered, 7 to 10 minutes or until all water is absorbed and bulgur is soft. Set aside, covered for a few minutes.
❷ Heat the remaining 1 tablespoon olive oil in a medium-sized skillet over moderate heat. Add the garlic and cook until golden.

Add the zucchini, reduce heat, cover, and cook for 5 minutes or until zucchini is tender. Uncover and cook for a minute or two so that any liquid that has accumulated at the bottom evaporates.

❸ Place the bulgur mixture, the garlic-zucchini mixture, and basil in a food processor. Pulse on and off several times until the ingredients are blended. Scrape into a large bowl. Add the sun-dried tomatoes, ground pine nuts, and 1½ cups of the bread crumbs. Mix with a large spoon or, even better, with your hands, until all ingredients are thoroughly combined. Season to taste with salt and pepper. Form into ½ inch thick patties 3 inches in diameter, mixing in extra bread crumbs if the patties don't hold their shape. The patties will be fragile, so handle them gently.

❹ Prepare a grill or preheat the broiler. If using a charcoal grill, see page 11 for instructions. Place the patties on a vegetable grid. If broiling, place the patties on a broiler pan or large cookie sheet lined with a lightly oiled piece of aluminum foil dusted with bread crumbs. Grill or broil 3 to 5 inches from the heat, 8 to 10 minutes per side or until lightly browned. (When one side is done, turn the patties carefully with a spatula.) Check often to prevent burning.

➤ *Serving Suggestions:* Serve on a warm garlic roll with basil leaves, tomato slices, and Indian ketchup. Enjoy the wine-glazed mushrooms on the side. These patties may also be served as an entrée with polenta and baked acorn or butternut squash. A salad of shredded napa cabbage dressed with Lime Vinaigrette (page 94) and topped with garlic croutons is an excellent first course. A bowl of red grapes will conclude the meal nicely.

➤ **PATTY MELT:** For those who fancy cheese burgers, here's an idea for a "melt." Prepare the burgers following the instructions above. Place a slice of Cheddar or another cheese of your choice on top and broil until cheese melts.

WINTER SQUASH
AND PUMPKIN SEED
BURGERS

inter squash and pumpkin seeds, the two major ingredients in this burger, are both indigenous to America, but the seasonings of lush, sensuous yellow curry paste and shredded coconut originate in Thailand. Crisp spears of sautéed asparagus add a touch of elegance to these spicy, faintly sweet burgers.

Makes 9 burgers, 4 servings

1½ pounds winter squash
(acorn, butternut, buttercup,
or the like), unpeeled
½ cup quinoa, rinsed
several times
1 tablespoon canola oil
1 cup diced onion
1 medium green bell pepper,
cored, seeded, and
coarsely chopped
2 teaspoons Thai yellow
curry paste
3 tablespoons sweetened
shredded or flaked coconut
½ cup shelled, raw pumpkin
seeds, toasted and ground to
a coarse powder in a
spice/coffee grinder

1½ cups Bread Crumbs
(page 7) or commercial
bread crumbs
Salt

CONDIMENT SUGGESTIONS
(Choose from one or more
of the following):
Shredded green leaf lettuce
Sweet onion slices
Honey-Ginger Mustard
(page 111)

❶ Preheat oven to 450 degrees.

❷ Halve or quarter the squash (depending on size) and scrape out the seeds. Place the squash pieces on an ungreased baking sheet, skin side down. Bake until the flesh is tender and can be pierced easily with a fork, 20 to 35 minutes. (The timing will vary with the thickness of the pieces.) Scrape the flesh away from the

skin with a spoon and measure out 1 cup. Discard the skin.
(Retain the excess for later use.)

❸ Bring the quinoa and 1 cup water to a boil in a medium
saucepan. Cover and cook until all water is absorbed and quinoa is
light and fluffy, 10 to 15 minutes. Measure 1 cup. (Retain the
excess for later use.)

❹ Heat the canola oil in a medium skillet over moderate heat.
Cook the onion until it is wilted. Add the bell pepper and
curry paste and stir to distribute evenly. Reduce heat and cook,
covered, 5 to 8 minutes or until the pepper is tender. Add the
squash. Cook, uncovered, for 3 to 5 minutes, stirring constantly.
Add the coconut and mix well. Remove from heat.

❺ Process the quinoa and the onion-squash mixture in a food
processor until well blended. Transfer to a large bowl. Add
the ground pumpkin seeds and 1 cup of the bread crumbs. Mix
with a large spoon or, even better, with your hands, until all
ingredients are thoroughly combined. Season to taste with salt.
Form into patties 3 inches in diameter and ½ inch thick, mixing
in extra bread crumbs if the patties don't hold their shape.

❻ Prepare a grill or preheat the broiler. If using a charcoal grill,
see page 11 for instructions. Place patties on a vegetable grid.
If broiling, place the patties on a broiler pan or large cookie sheet
lined with a lightly oiled piece of aluminum foil. Grill or broil
3 to 5 inches from the heat, 5 to 7 minutes per side or until
lightly browned. (When one side is done, turn the patties carefully
with a spatula.) Check often to prevent burning.

➤ *Serving Suggestions:* Serve burger-style on warmed sourdough
bread with shredded lettuce, onion slices, honey-ginger mustard,
and accompanied by Sautéed Asparagus or Gai Lan (page 88).
Or, serve as an entrée with couscous, steamed pea pods brushed
with dark sesame oil, and coleslaw.

TOFU AND OTHER SOY BURGERS

Soybean derivatives, especially tofu and tempeh, form such a marvelous base for burgers and are so nutritionally important to vegetarians that I have given them a chapter of their own. I was first introduced to soy foods through the cuisines of East Asia, where they are a part of the daily diet. Tofu appears most commonly in stir-fries and soups throughout the region, and tempeh in Indonesian salads, curries, and stir-fries. Later, I found that both make an excellent foundation for vegetarian burgers. And because of their complete protein content, they can take the place of meat.

Tofu, which is made from soy milk curds, has a neutral taste. It readily takes on the flavor of other ingredients during the cooking process, providing a canvas for an infinitely varied palette of seasonings such as cumin, ketchup, or sambal oelek. Like potato, tofu can be mashed to a smooth mixture that combines with grains, vegetables, and nuts to produce tasty, nutritious burgers. I happen to like tofu, but even those who don't fancy it are unlikely to be offended by its presence in these patties.

On occasion I smoke tofu, using a stovetop smoker. This technique infuses it with a rich smoky flavor reminiscent of traditional barbecued hamburger. The extra step increases the preparation time by 15 to 25 minutes, but is well worth the effort.

Tempeh, another form of soybean cake, is an excellent vegetable source of protein and one of the few vegetable sources of vitamin B_{12}. Unlike tofu, however, it has an assertive, musky flavor that puts some people off and can be a challenge to prepare. I tame it by poaching it in vegetable broth and/or sautéing it before using in recipes. Either method will mellow it somewhat, while retaining its characteristic flavor and the slightly chewy texture that make it a valuable ingredient in vegetarian burgers.

Whole soybeans take several hours of precooking, so I don't use them in burgers. Other soy foods such as tamari, soy sauce, and hoisin sauce are used throughout this book as flavoring agents.

Rich in taste and nutrition, the burger recipes below extend the use of soy foods beyond the traditional world of stir-fries and soups.

ROASTED EGGPLANT
AND TOFU BURGERS

ggplant, with its delicate texture, is difficult to use as a primary ingredient in vegetarian burgers. However, when combined with tofu and sweet bell pepper, it produces exquisite patties with a sensuous, silky texture. Wheat germ helps to firm up the mixture and boost nutrition, yet doesn't advertise its presence. These burgers are slow-baked, rather than grilled or broiled.

Makes 12 burgers, 6 servings

1 pound eggplant (1 medium), halved lengthwise
1 tablespoon olive oil
1½ cups finely chopped scallions
1 medium-sized red bell pepper, cored, seeded, and finely chopped
1 (14-ounce) carton firm tofu, drained, rinsed, and cut into 1-inch cubes
3 tablespoons smoky barbecue sauce
½ cup shelled, raw pumpkin seeds, toasted and ground to a coarse powder in a spice/coffee grinder
1 cup toasted wheat germ
1¾ cups Bread Crumbs (page 7) or commercial bread crumbs
Salt and freshly ground black pepper

CONDIMENT SUGGESTIONS
(Choose from one or more of the following):
Large red leaf lettuce leaves
Sweet onion slices
Two-Pepper Spread (page 115)

❶ Preheat the broiler.
❷ Arrange the eggplant halves, flat side down, on a cookie sheet lined with a piece of aluminum foil. Broil until the flesh softens, the skin chars, and a smoky aroma becomes noticeable, 10 or more minutes. (The timing will vary with the size and thickness of the eggplant.) Check often, as overbroiling will make the flesh dry. Allow to cool to room temperature. Remove the skin and discard. Coarsely chop the flesh.

❸ Heat the olive oil in a large skillet over moderate heat. Add scallions and bell pepper and stir several times. Add the reserved eggplant, tofu, and barbecue sauce. Cook, covered, to blend the flavors, 10 to 12 minutes. With a slotted spoon remove the tofu and vegetables and place in a large bowl. Reduce the sauce remaining in the skillet over medium heat to a thick, syrupy consistency, stirring often. This will take a few minutes. Pour over the tofu mixture.

❹ Preheat the oven to 425 degrees. Cover a large baking sheet with a piece of aluminum foil. Oil the foil lightly and dust with bread crumbs.

❺ Place the tofu-eggplant mixture in a food processor. Pulse on and off several times until the ingredients are thoroughly blended. Transfer to a large bowl. Add the ground pumpkin seeds, wheat germ, and 1 cup of the bread crumbs. Mix with a large spoon or, even better, with your hands, until all ingredients are thoroughly combined. Season to taste with salt and pepper. Form into patties 3 inches in diameter and ½ inch thick, mixing in extra bread crumbs if the patties don't hold their shape. They will be fragile, so handle them gently.

❻ Place the patties on the baking sheet. Bake for 30 minutes or until they are thoroughly heated and the tops are lightly browned.

➢ *Serving Suggestions:* Serve each burger wrapped in a large lettuce leaf (or on bread of your choice), with onion slivers and two-pepper spread. Alternatively, serve these patties as an entrée with mashed potatoes, grilled fresh corn, and Indian Ketchup (page 119).

TERIYAKI TOFU BURGERS

*I*hese burgers, a mixture of tofu, leafy greens, and yellow
vegetables, flavored with teriyaki sauce, are a complete meal on
their own. The teriyaki flavor may get muted from the cooking
process, so be sure to pass teriyaki sauce at the table to drizzle over
the burgers according to taste.

Makes 10 burgers, 5 servings

1 tablespoon canola oil
1 tablespoon minced garlic
½ of a 14-ounce carton firm
   tofu, drained, rinsed,
   dried between layers of
   paper towels, and cut into
   1-inch cubes
1½ cups (firmly packed)
   coarsely chopped beet
   greens or red chard,
   stems removed
¼ pound carrots, grated
   (slightly over 1 firmly
   packed cup)
3 tablespoons teriyaki sauce
2 teaspoons sugar

1 large egg or 2 egg whites
   (optional)
½ cup walnuts, toasted and
   ground to a coarse powder
   in a spice/coffee grinder
1¼ cups Bread Crumbs
   (page 7) or commercial
   bread crumbs
Salt

CONDIMENT SUGGESTIONS
(Choose from one or more
   of the following):
Radish slices
Peeled cucumber slices
Sweet onion slices

❶ Heat the canola oil in a medium skillet over moderate heat.
Add the garlic and cook until it is golden. Reduce heat. Add the
tofu, greens, carrots, and 2 tablespoons of the teriyaki sauce.
Cook, covered, 5 to 8 minutes or until the vegetables are tender
but still retain their color. Remove from heat and allow to cool to
room temperature.

❷ Place the tofu-vegetable mixture, the remaining 1 tablespoon
teriyaki sauce, sugar, and the optional egg or egg whites in a food
processor. Pulse on and off several times to blend the ingredients,

scraping the sides once. The mixture need not be completely smooth. Transfer to a large bowl. Add the ground walnuts and ½ cup of the bread crumbs. Mix with a large spoon or, even better, with your hands, until all ingredients are thoroughly combined. Season to taste with salt. Form into patties 3 inches in diameter and ½ inch thick, mixing in extra bread crumbs if the patties don't hold their shape. They will be delicate, so handle them gently.

❸ Prepare a grill or preheat the broiler. If using a charcoal grill, see page 11 for instructions. Place the patties on a vegetable grid. If broiling, place the patties on a broiler pan or large cookie sheet lined with a lightly oiled piece of aluminum foil dusted with bread crumbs. Grill or broil 3 to 5 inches from the heat, 5 to 7 minutes per side or until medium brown. (When one side is done, turn carefully with a spatula.) Check often to prevent burning.

➤ *Serving Suggestions:* Serve on toasted black olive bread (or buns of your choice), garnished with radish, cucumber, and onion slices. A side dish of Onion–Apple Rings (page 89) adds a nice touch; a mixed green salad moistened with Lime Vinaigrette (page 94) will round out the meal. Or, savor these patties as an entrée with brown basmati rice and Sautéed Asparagus or Gai Lan (page 88); Zippy Buttermilk Soup (page 100) makes an excellent starter.

TOFU AND OTHER
SOY BURGERS

SMOKED TOFU AND
HAZELNUT BURGERS

Smoking tofu prior to using it in burger recipes improves its *flavor and reduces its moisture content, enabling it to absorb the flavor of other ingredients better. A stovetop smoker works well for this purpose. I often smoke more tofu than I need for the burger recipe and use the surplus in other dishes. (Store this excess tofu in the refrigerator.) Here the richly smoked tofu is combined with mushrooms and hazelnuts to create these superlative burgers.*

Makes 10 burgers, 5 servings

1 (14-ounce) carton firm tofu, drained, rinsed, dried between layers of paper towels, and cut into 1-inch cubes
1 tablespoon canola oil
3 to 5 large garlic cloves, minced
1 medium-sized red bell pepper, cored, seeded, and coarsely chopped
½ pound fresh mushrooms, sliced ¼ inch thick
1 tablespoon tamari
1 cup cooked white basmati rice, preferably (or other long-grain white rice)

1 tablespoon dark sesame oil
¼ cup hazelnuts, toasted and ground to a coarse powder in a spice/coffee grinder
1¾ cups Bread Crumbs (page 7) or commercial bread crumbs
Salt and freshly ground black pepper

CONDIMENT SUGGESTIONS
(Choose one or both of the following):
Chipotle Ketchup (page 120)
Five Fresh Aromatics (page 126)

❶ Smoke tofu in a stovetop smoker according to the manufacturer's directions. Check after 15 minutes. If the smoky flavor is still faint, smoke longer, an additional 10 to 15 minutes, or to your taste. Allow to cool.

❷ Heat the canola oil in a large skillet over moderate heat. Cook the garlic until it is golden. Add the bell pepper, mushrooms, and tamari and mix well. Reduce heat, cover, and cook until the vegetables are tender, 5 to 8 minutes. With a slotted spoon, remove the vegetables to a large bowl. Cook the sauce remaining in the skillet over medium heat, stirring occasionally, until it is reduced to a thick, syrupy consistency, a few minutes. Pour over the vegetables.

❸ Process the tofu, bell pepper–mushroom mixture, and rice in a food processor until thoroughly blended. Scrape into a large bowl. Add the sesame oil, ground hazelnuts, and 1 cup of the bread crumbs. Mix with a large spoon or, even better, with your hands, until all ingredients are thoroughly combined. Season to taste with salt and pepper. Form into patties 3 inches in diameter and ½ inch thick, mixing in extra bread crumbs if the patties don't hold their shape.

❹ Prepare a grill or preheat the broiler. If using a charcoal grill, see page 11 for instructions. Place the patties on a vegetable grid. If broiling, place the patties on a broiler pan or large cookie sheet lined with a lightly oiled piece of aluminum foil. Grill or broil 3 to 5 inches from the heat, 7 to 10 minutes per side or until lightly browned. (When one side is done, turn carefully with a spatula.) Check often to prevent burning.

➤ *Serving Suggestions:* Try these on toasted potato bread with chipotle ketchup and five fresh aromatics. Serve Coconut Sambal (page 118) on the side. Alternatively, serve the patties as an entrée with wild rice, baked acorn or butternut squash topped with Two-Cheese Spread (page 116), and Wilted Baby Greens (page 96). In season, a plate of fresh plums or cherries makes a lovely dessert.

TOFU AND OTHER
SOY BURGERS

TEMPEH WALNUT BURGERS

 *deep, shiny cherry glaze coats these fine-textured burgers with their faint hint of tempeh flavor.*

Makes 10 burgers, 5 servings

1 (8-ounce) package
soy tempeh, cut into
1-inch cubes
½ cup vegetable broth
2 tablespoons canola oil
¼ teaspoon dark sesame oil
1 pound yams, peeled and cut
into 1-inch cubes
3 to 5 large garlic cloves,
coarsely chopped
2 medium-sized red bell
peppers, cored, seeded, and
coarsely chopped
1 jalapeño pepper or other fresh
green chile, cored, seeded,
and minced (or to taste)
2 tablespoons vegetarian oyster
sauce or hoisin sauce

¼ cup walnuts, toasted and
ground to a coarse powder
in a spice/coffee grinder
1½ cups Bread Crumbs
(page 7) or commercial
bread crumbs
Salt

CONDIMENT SUGGESTIONS
(Choose from one or more
of the following):
Shredded daikon or cucumber
slices
Shredded romaine lettuce
Sweet onion slices
Cherry Glaze (page 125)
Kimchi (Korean pickled
vegetable, available in
Asian markets)

❶ Bring the tempeh and broth to a boil in a medium saucepan over moderate heat. Reduce heat. Simmer, covered, 3 to 5 minutes or until tempeh is puffy. Drain, discarding liquid, if any. Allow to cool. Mash tempeh thoroughly with a fork.

❷ Heat 1 tablespoon of the canola oil in a medium skillet over moderate heat. Add the tempeh. Reduce heat and cook, uncovered, for a few minutes, stirring often. Stir in the sesame oil. Remove from the heat and reserve.

❸ Steam the yams until tender, 15 to 20 minutes. Remove from heat and allow to cool. Mash thoroughly with a fork. Heat the remaining 1 tablespoon canola oil in a medium skillet over moderate heat. Add the garlic and cook until it is golden. Add the bell peppers and jalapeño. Reduce heat and cook, covered, until the bell peppers are tender, 6 to 8 minutes. Add the mashed yams and vegetarian oyster sauce or hoisin sauce. Cook, uncovered, for a few minutes, stirring to mix well. Remove from the heat.

❹ Place the reserved tempeh and the yam-bell pepper mixture in a food processor. Process until the mixture is reduced to a smooth purée. Transfer to a large bowl. Add the ground walnuts and 1 cup of the bread crumbs. Mix with a large spoon or, even better, with your hands, until all ingredients are thoroughly combined. Season to taste with salt. Form into 3-inch patties about ½ inch thick, mixing in extra bread crumbs if the patties don't hold their shape. They will be delicate, so handle them gently.

❺ Prepare a grill or preheat the broiler. If using a charcoal grill, see page 11 for instructions. Place patties on a vegetable grid. If broiling, place the patties on a broiler pan or large cookie sheet lined with a lightly oiled piece of aluminum foil. Grill or broil 3 to 5 inches from the heat, 8 to 11 minutes per side or until lightly browned. (When one side is done, turn carefully with a spatula.) Check often to prevent burning.

➤ *Serving Suggestions:* Slide each burger into a pita half and add daikon, romaine, onion slices, and cherry glaze. Serve kimchi (optionally) on the side. Alternatively, try as an entrée with kasha cooked in vegetable broth and topped with Caramelized Onion (page 113), Wine-glazed Mushrooms (page 101), and a mixed green salad with orange segments.

TOFU AND OTHER
SOY BURGERS

VEGETARIAN
SLOPPY JOE

n this vegetarian version of the all-American favorite, tempeh takes the place of ground meat. If you are new to tempeh, this is an easy first dish to try.

3 to 4 servings

1 (8-ounce) package
   soy tempeh, cut into
   1-inch cubes
1 tablespoon smoky
   barbecue sauce
1 tablespoon hoisin sauce
¾ teaspoon sambal oelek, if
   available; or ground red
   pepper to taste

2 tablespoons olive oil
1 cup minced onion
¼ pound tomatoes
   (1 medium), peeled and
   coarsely chopped
Salt

CONDIMENT SUGGESTION
Indian Ketchup (page 119)

❶ Steam the tempeh until puffy, about 5 minutes. Using a fork, mash the tempeh thoroughly. Add the barbecue sauce, hoisin sauce, and sambal oelek and mix well.

❷ Heat the olive oil in a large skillet over moderate heat. Add onion and cook until the edges turn brown, stirring continuously. Add the mashed tempeh and tomato. Reduce heat and cook, uncovered, stirring constantly to blend the flavors, 5 to 7 minutes. Add salt to taste.

➤ *Serving Suggestions:* Serve atop toasted garlic rolls drizzled with Indian ketchup. Sautéed Asparagus Gai Lan (page 88) and Wine-glazed Mushrooms (page 101) are two flavorful dishes worth considering as accompaniments.

STUFFED BURGERS

PEA AND CARROT–FILLED CUTLETS   72

ONION-FILLED KIBBES   75

SHIITAKE-STUFFED BARLEY BURGERS   78

KALE STUFFING   80

EGG-ALMOND STUFFING   80

PEANUT STUFFING   81

*I*n my native India, stuffed vegetable patties announce a special occasion. Their preparation is elaborate, as befits such events. Most ingredients are prepared from scratch. Cooked potatoes, mashed by hand, are almost always used to form the outer shells, which are usually filled with whole hard-boiled eggs, but occasionally with spicy vegetables, chutneys, or minced beets for added color. The oval-shaped patties are rolled in bread crumbs, fried, and served alone as a special course. That way the diners can enjoy them, especially their surprise filling, without being distracted by other dishes.

When preparing stuffed burgers in my American kitchen, I vary the shell ingredients. Among my favorites are carrots or sweet potatoes as well as a variety of cooked grains, such as rice or barley. A food processor makes it a snap to grind the ingredients to the right consistency. Instead of using a whole cooked egg as a filling, which will almost double the size of the burgers and make them difficult to handle, I opt for a mixture of chopped cooked eggs and pine nuts. I can't escape my Indian heritage, however, so I also like to use spicy vegetable fillings. But I am equally at home with less fiery alternatives: caramelized onion, minced scallions, whole roasted garlic cloves, or sautéed mushrooms. All work wonderfully well.

The recipes presented below are the ones I've found especially suitable for stuffing, but you need not stop there. Most burger recipes in this book work quite well with a variety of stuffings. I have listed a few basic ideas at the end of this chapter. If time doesn't allow for preparing a more elaborate filling, tuck a spoonful of chopped toasted almonds and raisins into the middle of the burger.

Experiment and have fun with stuffings, only make sure that the stuffing ingredients are either minced or spreadable. Stuff any burger recipe in this book, not just the ones mentioned in this chapter. Add extra bread crumbs if necessary to make the patties firmer so they will hold together with the added weight of the filling.

Whether simple or elaborate, these stuffed burgers will add a new dimension to your dining experience.

PEA AND CARROT-FILLED CUTLETS

ashed sweet potatoes mixed with rice and mushrooms make a wonderful outer shell for stuffed burgers. The spicy pea and carrot stuffing is good on its own as a snack or side dish.

Makes 8 stuffed burgers, 4 servings

FILLING

½ pound carrots, finely chopped (about 2 cups)

1 cup fresh or thawed frozen peas

1 tablespoon plus 2 teaspoons canola oil

1 tablespoon plus 2 teaspoons minced garlic

2 teaspoons kofta masala (see Note)

2 tablespoons raisins

1 tablespoon slivered almonds

Salt

SHELLS

½ pound sweet potatoes, peeled and cut into ½-inch-thick slices (about 2 cups)

½ pound fresh mushrooms, sliced ¼ inch thick

1 cup cooked white basmati rice or other long-grain white rice

1 large egg or 2 egg whites (optional)

¼ cup pine nuts, toasted and ground to a coarse powder in a spice/coffee grinder

2 cups Bread Crumbs (page 7) or commercial bread crumbs

Salt

Dash ground red pepper, or to taste

CONDIMENT SUGGESTIONS (Choose from one or more of the following):

Shredded green leaf lettuce

Raw, sweet onion rings

Mango pickles (available in Indian groceries; optional) or supermarket mango chutney

Cucumber-Basil Raita (page 124)

❶ To make the filling, steam the carrots until tender, 8 to 10 minutes. Set aside. Steam fresh peas until tender, 5 to 7 minutes. (Thawed frozen peas will not require extra cooking.)

❷ Heat 2 teaspoons of the canola oil in a small skillet over moderate heat. Add 2 teaspoons of the garlic and cook until golden. Add kofta masala and 1 tablespoon water and stir until well distributed. Add carrots, peas, raisins, and almonds. Cook, uncovered, about 5 minutes, mashing the peas and carrots with the back of a spoon. Season to taste with salt. Remove from heat and allow to cool.

❸ For the shells, steam the sweet potatoes until they can be pierced easily with a fork, 15 to 18 minutes. Allow to cool to room temperature. Heat the remaining 1 tablespoon of canola oil in a medium skillet over moderate heat. Add the remaining 1 tablespoon of garlic and cook until golden. Add the mushrooms. Cook, covered, until the mushrooms are tender, about 5 minutes. Remove garlic-mushroom mixture with a slotted spoon and place in a bowl.

Reduce the liquid left in the skillet to about a tablespoon by cooking uncovered over medium-low heat for a few minutes or until slightly thickened. Pour over the garlic-mushroom-mixture.

❹ Place the sweet potatoes, garlic-mushroom mixture, rice, and the optional egg or egg whites in the container of a food processor. Pulse on and off several times until the ingredients are thoroughly blended. Transfer to a large bowl and add the ground pine nuts and 1¼ cups of the bread crumbs. Mix with a spoon, or, even better, with your hands, until the ingredients are thoroughly combined.

Season to taste with salt and red pepper. Shape into 16 patties, 3 inches in diameter and between ¼ and ½ inch thick, mixing in extra bread crumbs if the patties don't hold their shape. (Dust your palms with bread crumbs, as the balls will be sticky.) Place one patty on a board and spread 2 tablespoons of the peas-and-carrots filling over it, leaving a border of about ½ inch all around. Place another patty on top. Pinch the edges together. Prepare the remaining patties the same way.

❺ Prepare a grill or preheat the broiler. If using a charcoal grill, see page 11 for instructions. Place the patties on a vegetable grid. If broiling, place the patties on a broiler pan or large cookie sheet lined with a lightly oiled piece of aluminum foil. Grill or broil 3 to 5 inches from the heat, 5 to 8 minutes per side or until the top is light to medium brown in color. (When one side is done, gently turn the patties with a spatula.) Check often to prevent burning.

➤ *Note:* Kofta masala is a ground spice mix sold in Indian groceries and contains 7 or more spices, including cumin, red pepper, coriander, and bay leaf. If it is not available, use a supermarket curry powder, or in a pinch, a mixture of 2 teaspoons ground cumin, ¼ teaspoon ground turmeric, and ground red pepper to taste. These burgers taste best if slightly chile-hot.

➤ *Serving Suggestions:* Slide each patty into a halved pita bread along with lettuce, onion, a bit of mango pickle, and a dollop of cucumber-basil raita. Serve any leftover filling on the side or refrigerate for later use as a snack. These patties make a satisfying main course served with quinoa or couscous and accompanied by steamed beets and cauliflower. Two-Cheese Spread (page 116) makes a nice sauce. The patties also work well as an appetizer. In this case, skip the filling and roll into 1½-inch balls; grill or broil them and serve with Date-Raisin Chutney (page 121).

ONION-FILLED
KIBBES

his recipe is inspired by the Middle Eastern dish kibbe or khuba. Traditionally, the Middle Eastern cooks spent hours preparing the shells, a pounded mixture of cracked wheat and ground meat, then filling them with a spicy meat-nut mixture. Here potatoes replace the meat, but you get a similar nutty, chewy texture from bulgur (finely ground cracked wheat). The filling, a layer of cheese and sweet onion, provides a pleasant creamy contrast.

Makes 8 stuffed burgers, 4 servings

½ cup fat-free cream cheese
1 cup minced sweet onion
¾ pound potatoes, peeled and cut into 1-inch cubes
1 tablespoon canola oil
3 to 5 large garlic cloves, minced
¼ teaspoon ground turmeric
¼ pound fresh mushrooms, sliced ¼ inch thick
Salt
1 teaspoon tamarind concentrate
1 teaspoon garam masala
½ cup prepared Bulgur (page 8)

1 large egg or 2 egg whites (optional)
¼ cup walnuts, toasted and ground to a coarse powder in a spice/coffee grinder
1½ cups Bread Crumbs (page 7) or commercial bread crumbs

CONDIMENT SUGGESTIONS
(Choose from one or more of the following):
Shredded romaine lettuce
Peeled, thinly sliced cucumber
Chipotle Ketchup (page 120)

❶ Combine the cream cheese and onion in a medium bowl and stir with a fork until smooth.
❷ Steam potatoes until tender, 15 to 20 minutes. Allow them to cool, then mash thoroughly.
❸ Heat the canola oil in a large skillet over moderate heat. Cook the garlic until it is golden. Stir in the turmeric. Add the

mushrooms. Cook, covered, for 3 to 5 few minutes or until the mushrooms are tender. Add the mashed potatoes. Now add salt, tamarind, and garam masala and mix well. Cook, uncovered, for 2 more minutes to blend the flavors, stirring often. Remove from heat and allow to cool.

❹ Place the potato-mushroom mixture, bulgur, and the optional egg or egg whites in a food processor. Pulse on and off several times until the mixture is thoroughly blended. Transfer to a large bowl and add the ground walnuts and 1 cup of the bread crumbs. Mix with a spoon or, even better, with your hands, until all ingredients are thoroughly combined. Season to taste with salt.

❺ Shape into balls, then flatten each to a 3-inch patty about ¼ inch thick. This is best done by placing the patty on a cutting board and pressing with your fingers. Place a tablespoon of the cream cheese–onion mixture on top of a patty, spreading it evenly, leaving a ½-inch border all the way around. Place another patty of equal size on top. Pinch the edges together, making sure no filling escapes. (The thinner you can roll the patties and the more stuffing you can put in, the better the burgers will taste. However, as they become thinner, they often become more delicate and difficult to handle.) Repeat the process with all the patties. (The traditional manner of filling the kibbe is by making a hollow in the ball with your finger and inserting a small amount of filling. Close it carefully and roll it between the palms of your hands to make it smooth. Flatten it carefully so the filling doesn't show. In this case, only a small amount of filling can be used.)

❻ Prepare a grill or preheat the broiler. If using a charcoal grill, see page 11 for instructions. Place the patties on a vegetable grid. If broiling, place patties on a broiler pan or large cookie sheet lined with a lightly oiled piece of aluminum foil dusted with bread crumbs. Grill or broil 3 to 5 inches from the heat,

5 to 7 minutes per side or until lightly browned. (When one side is done, gently turn the patties to the other side with a spatula.) Check often to prevent burning

➤ *Serving Suggestions:* Try on a toasted bread of your choice with lettuce, cucumber, and chipotle ketchup. Sautéed Asparagus or Gai Lan (page 88) is wonderful served on the side. To serve as a main course, arrange the patties on a bed of quinoa and accompany with Double-Garlic Potatoes (page 92). Kibbes are traditionally served with a dairy-based dish, so start the meal with Zippy Buttermilk Soup (page 100) or accompany with Cucumber-Basil Raita (page 124).

➤**WHOLE MILLET COATING:** For extra nutrition, crunch, and visual appeal pat a few kernels of millet on both sides of each stuffed patty at the end of Step 3.

SHIITAKE-STUFFED
BARLEY BURGERS

ooked barley mixed with mashed sweet potato is a marvelous foundation for stuffed burgers. Mushrooms are traditional accompaniments to barley. Spicy-tart rasam *powder, a mixture of several ground spices from South India, lends a savory touch to these stuffed grain-and-vegetable burgers.*

Makes 7 stuffed burgers, 3 to 4 servings

½ cup pearl barley
1 pound sweet potatoes, peeled
   and cut into 1-inch cubes
1 tablespoon canola oil
1 cup diced onion
1 cup minced celery
1½ teaspoons rasam powder
   (see Note)
¼ to ½ cup vegetable broth

2 cups Bread Crumbs
   (page 7) or commercial
   bread crumbs
Wine-glazed Mushrooms
   (page 101)
CONDIMENT SUGGESTIONS
(Choose one or both of
   the following):
Shredded red cabbage
Basil "Mayonnaise" (page 116)

❶ Bring the barley and 2 cups water to a boil in a medium saucepan. Reduce heat, cover, and cook until all water is absorbed and barley is tender to the bite, about 45 minutes. Measure 1 cup. (Retain the excess for later use.)

❷ Steam the sweet potatoes until tender, 15 to 18 minutes. Mash thoroughly.

❸ Heat the canola oil in a large skillet over moderate heat. Add the onion and cook until it is medium brown, 7 to 10 minutes, stirring often. (Watch carefully and don't let it burn.) Add the celery and rasam powder and stir to distribute evenly. Add ¼ cup of the broth. Reduce heat and simmer, covered, 3 to 5 minutes, or until celery is softer. Add the mashed sweet potatoes. Cook, uncovered, for about 5 minutes, stirring continuously.

❹ Place the cooked barley and the sweet potato mixture in a food processor and process to a smooth purée. Transfer to a large bowl. Add 1½ cups of the bread crumbs, mix thoroughly, and season to taste with salt. Pinch off two balls, each slightly larger than a walnut. Roll them in your palms to make them smooth. Flatten each into a patty 3 inches in diameter and ¼ inch thick. (This can be done by placing them on a board and pressing them with your palm.) Place a tablespoon of wine-glazed mushroom filling on one of them, spreading it evenly across the surface and leaving a ½-inch border all the way around. Put the second patty on top. Pinch their edges together, making sure no filling escapes. Prepare the rest of the mixture the same way.

❺ Prepare a grill or preheat the broiler. If using a charcoal grill, see page 11 for instructions. Place patties on a vegetable grid. If broiling, place the patties on a broiler pan or large cookie sheet lined with a lightly oiled piece of aluminum foil. Grill or broil 3 to 5 inches from the heat, 6 to 9 minutes per side or until the top looks set and is slightly darker in color. (When one side is done, turn carefully with a spatula.) Check often to prevent burning.

➤ *Note:* Rasam powder, available in Indian grocery stores, is a ground mixture of coriander seeds, black mustard seeds, red pepper, cumin, and other spices. You can substitute curry powder, but the taste will not be the same.

➤ *Serving Suggestions:* Serve on toasted bread of your choice with shredded red cabbage and basil "mayonnaise." Country Salad (page 97) is an appropriate accompaniment. As an entrée, serve with baked potatoes topped with Salsa International (page 123) and a platter of radishes, black olives, and cucumber.

KALE STUFFING

Stuffs 6 burgers

1 tablespoon dark sesame oil
About ¼ pound finely minced
  kale (enough to make
  3 firmly packed cups)
1 teaspoon chile paste with
  garlic or sambal oelek (both
  available in Asian markets)

½ teaspoon tamari
Salt and freshly ground
  black pepper

Heat the sesame oil in a medium skillet over moderate heat.
Add the kale, chile paste, and tamari. Reduce heat and simmer,
covered, 7 to 10 minutes until the kale is tender but retains
its color. Season to taste with salt and pepper. Remove from heat
and allow to cool.

EGG-ALMOND
STUFFING

*his stuffing is easy to work with and provides a nice textural
contrast to the burger.*

Stuffs 6 to 8 burgers

3 large hard-cooked eggs,
  sliced into ½-inch
  thick rounds

3 tablespoons slivered almonds
Salt and freshly ground black
  pepper (optional)

Stuff each burger with 2 to 3 egg slices, a few almond slivers, and
a dusting of salt and pepper.

PEANUT STUFFING

eanut fanciers love to find this creamy peanut filling
with crunchy onion in the center of their favorite vegetarian burger.

Stuffs 6 burgers

Peanut Sauce (page 112;   1 cup minced sweet onion
  prepared without
  addition of water)

Combine peanut sauce and onion in a large bowl.

➤**SHORTCUT STUFFING IDEAS:** Here are some quick,
easy-to-prepare fillings for those times when you're in a hurry.
They may be used individually or combined according to your
taste.
  • Sautéed, minced garlic (by itself or in combination with
    hoisin sauce and plum sauce)
  • Minced scallions or chives
  • Cooked beans of any type, crushed and seasoned
  • Shredded sweet coconut and raisins
  • Crumbly goat cheese
  • Drained and chopped olives, capers, or pickles (sweet or dill)
  • Commercial chutneys (from supermarkets) or small amounts
    of pickles from Indian food shops

S I D E

D I S H E S

THREE-PEPPER SAUTÉ 87

SAUTÉED ASPARAGUS OR GAI LAN 88

ONION-APPLE RINGS 89

SUMMER SQUASH STIR-FRY 90

DOUBLE-GARLIC POTATOES 92

BEET SALAD WITH LIME AND PINE NUTS 93

LIME VINAIGRETTE 94

*t*o round out a burger meal, I select my side dishes carefully. These dishes need not be show-stoppers — the burgers should remain the featured attraction — but they should be substantial and complement the burgers in taste and texture. Well-chosen accompaniments also contribute important nutrients and make the meal more interesting.

To complement a tender burger, I often begin with a crunchy salad of bell peppers, sweet onions, and cucumbers. If the burgers are nutty and chewy, I serve them with smooth, waxy potatoes or succulent mushrooms. To temper a spicy vegetarian burger, I might rely on lightly steamed broccoli or cauliflower moistened with a hint of vinaigrette. When serving vegetarian burgers without a bun, I typically prepare a grain pilaf flavored with saffron and studded with peas, raisins, and toasted cashews. Rice, millet, quinoa, or couscous all make an excellent pilaf that serves as a bed for the burgers.

Whenever possible, I use fresh, seasonal ingredients and cook them minimally. During spring and summer, I grill zucchini, mushrooms, and bell peppers along with the burgers. Dark leafy greens such as Swiss chard, mustard greens, or beet greens appear on my table throughout the year.

They are highly nutritious, easy to prepare, and have a rich, succulent texture that goes well with any vegetarian burger. All of these side dishes are suitable for other meals as well, so leftovers are never a problem.

THREE-PEPPER
SAUTÉ

his bright, cheery sauté of red, green, and golden bell peppers adds a textural contrast and a rich, sweet accent to burger meals. The vegetables are cooked briefly so they will retain their juicy crunch. Green peppers alone will do, but when in season, the red and golden peppers provide a background sweetness without the slightly bitter aftertaste of the early-season, green version. Try this side dish with any vegetarian burger, alone or accompanied by sliced ripe tomatoes drizzled with balsamic vinegar and sprinkled with chopped fresh basil. Any leftovers make a perfect light meal paired with crostini or garlic bread.

3 to 4 side dish servings

1 tablespoon olive oil
1 cup thinly slivered onion
4 large bell peppers
   (a combination of red, green, and golden peppers, or green peppers alone), cored, seeded, and cut into 1-inch strips

¼ cup vegetable broth
1 to 2 teaspoons vegetarian oyster sauce or hoisin sauce to taste
Salt (optional)

Heat the oil in a large, steep-sided skillet over moderate heat. Add the onion and cook until it is translucent. Add the bell peppers, 1 tablespoon broth, and vegetarian oyster sauce. Reduce heat. Cover and cook for 1 to 2 minutes. Uncover and cook, stirring, for 4 to 6 minutes or just until the peppers are slightly tender, but still retain a little crunch. Stir in a little extra broth if the mixture begins to stick to the bottom of the skillet. Remove from heat. Taste and add salt if necessary and adjust the amount of vegetarian oyster sauce.

SAUTÉED ASPARAGUS OR GAI LAN

his recipe works equally well with asparagus tips or, in season, gai lan. Also known as Chinese broccoli, gai lan has slender flower stalks that resemble miniature heads of broccoli. The succulent vegetable has a pleasant, slightly bitter taste, somewhere between broccoli and mustard greens, and deserves to be better known.

3 to 4 small servings

2 teaspoons canola oil
2 large garlic cloves, minced
½ pound asparagus tips
   (top 3 inches only), or gai
   lan, cut into 3-inch sections

2 tablespoons to ¼ cup
   vegetable broth
Salt (optional)

Heat canola oil in a large skillet over moderate heat. Add the garlic and cook until it is golden. Add asparagus or gai lan and 2 tablespoons of the broth. Reduce heat. Simmer, covered, 5 to 8 minutes or just until the vegetables are crisp-tender, stirring in a little extra broth if all the liquid has evaporated and the mixture is beginning to dry out.

Remove from heat. Season to taste with salt if needed. Lift the vegetables with a slotted spoon and arrange attractively around the burgers on individual plates.

ONION-APPLE RINGS

ere apple and onion rings are sautéed gently, then dusted with a fragrant garam masala mix. A sprinkling of sugar produces a delicate, caramel effect without making the dish overly sweet. Served warm with any vegetarian burger, this is a taste treat.

4 small side dish servings

1 tablespoon olive oil
1 tablespoon butter (optional;
    for flavor)
1 cup sweet raw onion rings
    about ¼ inch thick
    (see Note)
1½ pounds tart apples
    (about 3), cored but not
    peeled, cut into ¼-inch-
    thick rings

1 to 2 teaspoons sugar,
    or to taste
½ teaspoon garam masala
Salt
1 tablespoon freshly squeezed
    lime juice

Heat the olive oil and butter in a large skillet over moderate heat. Cook onion until lightly browned, about 5 to 8 minutes, stirring often. Add the apple rings and sugar. Cook, uncovered, until the apples are tender but still hold their shape, 3 to 5 minutes, stirring continuously but gently, as the apple pieces will be fragile. Sprinkle on garam masala and stir to distribute evenly. Add salt to taste. Remove from heat. Sprinkle lime juice on top. Best served warm.

➤ *Note:* Red or other sweet onions such as Walla Walla, Vidalia, or Maui onions work better than regular yellow onions, which have a strong flavor.

SUMMER SQUASH
STIR-FRY

*h*ere *summer squash and red bell peppers make a*
succulent, colorful medley. I prefer scallop-edged pattypan squash,
either yellow or green, but zucchini also works. These squashes are
delicately flavored, so I toss them with slices of mild onion and a
drizzle of hoisin sauce, leaving out the stronger-tasting garlic. This
results in a light sauce that is spicy-sweet yet not overpowering.
Toasted slivered almonds decorate the finished dish. Don't overcook
this dish; it tastes best when the squash pieces are cooked through,
but are still firm with a bit of crunch.

4 side dish servings

1½ pounds pattypan squash or
    zucchini
1 tablespoon olive oil
1 cup thinly sliced onion
1½ teaspoons hoisin sauce

1 large red bell pepper, cored,
    seeded, and cut into thin strips
Salt (optional)
GARNISH
Toasted slivered almonds

❶ If using pattypan squash, cut each in half across the scalloped
edge. Lay each piece on a board with the cut side down and
slice into ½-inch-thick pieces. Wider pieces can be halved in the
middle. The end result should be pieces approximately
1½-inch squares, ½ inch thick. If using zucchini, slice each into
½-inch-thick rounds with the wider pieces in the middle
halved. Set aside.

❷ Heat the olive oil in a large skillet or wok over moderate heat.
Cook the onion until it is wilted. Add hoisin sauce and stir
to distribute it evenly. Add the reserved squash and the bell
pepper. Reduce heat slightly. Cover and cook until the vegetables
are fork-tender, 7 to 10 minutes. (The vegetables will cook in
their own liquid. Uncover occasionally to check. If the vegetables
are starting to stick to the bottom of the skillet, stir in a teaspoon
or two of water.) Test for doneness and remove any small pieces to

avoid overcooking. Season to taste with salt. The dish can be served at this point, or you can thicken the sauce. To do so, lift the vegetables with a slotted spoon and place on a heated serving platter. Cook the sauce remaining in the skillet, uncovered, over medium heat for a few minutes until it thickens to a near syrupy consistency, stirring occasionally. Pour the thickened sauce over the vegetables. Serve garnished with almonds.

DOUBLE-GARLIC
POTATOES

*m*any consider French fries to be an ideal companion
to burgers, but this potato dish containing much less oil is an equally
worthy partner. Double-garlic potatoes exude flavors of cumin and
*fresh chiles, and have an inviting, crusty-brown look. The nuance of
garlic comes from both fresh garlic and asafetida powder.*

4 side dish servings

1½ tablespoons mustard oil
   or canola oil
½ teaspoon asafetida powder
2 to 3 large garlic cloves,
   minced
½ teaspoon ground cumin
1½ pounds boiling potatoes,
   peeled or unpeeled, cut into
   1½-inch cubes

1 jalapeño pepper or other
   green chile of choice, cored,
   seeded, and minced (or to
   taste)
Salt

GARNISH

Finely chopped chives or
   scallions

Heat the mustard or canola oil in a large skillet over moderate
heat. Sprinkle asafetida over the oil. Add the garlic, cumin,
potatoes, and jalapeño. Cook, uncovered, until the potatoes turn
brown in places, 5 to 8 minutes, stirring often. Reduce heat,
add 3 tablespoons water, and cook, covered, until the potatoes can
be pierced easily with a toothpick, another 10 to 15 minutes.
Season to taste with salt. Best served immediately, garnished with
chives, but can also be served at room temperature.

➤**SUNDAY BURGER BUFFET:** For an easy, colorful
vegetarian buffet, serve a vegetarian burger of your choice
accompanied by these chunky potatoes, raw and steamed vegetables,
and an assortment of breads. Include your choice of trimmings, and
also consider one or more of the following condiments: Chipotle
Ketchup (page 120), Two-Cheese Spread (page 116), and Five Fresh
Aromatics (page 126).

BEET SALAD WITH LIME
AND PINE NUTS

chunky, succulent root vegetable such as beet need only be simply steamed to become a worthy complement for vegetarian burgers. Here steamed beets are cloaked in a faintly tart, lime-based vinaigrette to enhance their natural sweetness. Round out the dish by sprinkling with sesame oil and adding toasted pine nuts, feta cheese, and cilantro.

4 side dish servings

1½ pounds beets, peeled to
  remove root hairs if any, cut
  into 1-inch cubes
½ cup Lime Vinaigrette
  (recipe follows)
Lettuce leaves
Several dashes dark sesame oil,
  to taste

GARNISHES

Feta (or other crumbly
  goat cheese)
Toasted pine nuts
Cilantro

Steam the beets until fork-tender, 15 to 20 minutes. Immediately transfer to a large bowl and pour 3 tablespoons of lime vinaigrette over them. Toss gently to coat each piece, adding more dressing if desired. Best served immediately, but can be stored in the refrigerator for several hours. Before serving, mix in with the liquid that has accumulated at the bottom. Lift the beets with a slotted spoon and place on lettuce leaves that have been arranged on individual serving plates. Sprinkle with sesame oil and garnish with feta cheese, pine nuts, and cilantro.

LIME VINAIGRETTE

his dressing is also excellent with a salad of mixed greens and toasted walnuts.

Makes 1 cup, enough for 4 servings

½ cup extra-virgin olive oil or walnut oil
¼ cup balsamic vinegar
¼ cup freshly squeezed lime juice

1 teaspoon sugar
Salt

Combine the olive oil, vinegar, lime juice, and sugar in a screw-top jar. Close the jar and shake vigorously to thicken the dressing. Season to taste with salt. Shake again before serving.

GINGER AND WINE-
SAUCED
GREEN BEANS

*ere is a marvelous dish that requires little preparation.
Toss green beans in hot oil with a bit of ginger, rice wine,
and tamari, then decorate with toasted almonds or bread crumbs.*

4 side dish servings

1 tablespoon tamari
1 tablespoon mirin
    (Japanese rice wine)
½ teaspoon sugar
Dash ground red pepper,
    to taste
1 tablespoon olive oil
1 cup diced onion

1 tablespoon grated ginger root
1 pound green beans, ends
    trimmed, cut diagonally into
    1½-inch strips
Salt (optional)
GARNISH
Toasted sliced almonds or
    bread crumbs

❶ Combine the tamari, rice wine, sugar, and red pepper in a small
bowl. Set aside.

❷ Heat the olive oil in a large skillet over moderate heat. Add
the onion and ginger root and cook until the onion is wilted.
Reduce heat slightly. Add the tamari–rice wine mixture and green
beans. Simmer, covered, until the beans are fork-tender, 6 to 10
minutes. (The vegetables will cook in their own liquid. Check
periodically to ensure that the mixture is not beginning to stick
to the bottom of the skillet. If it does, stir in a tablespoon of
water.) The amount of salt and red pepper can be adjusted at this
time. (This dish tastes best if slightly chile-hot.) The small amount
of sauce that forms should be thick and clingy. If it is still a little
watery, remove the vegetables with a slotted spoon to a heated
serving plate and keep covered. Cook the sauce remaining in the
skillet, uncovered, over medium-low heat for a few minutes until
it thickens, stirring often. Pour the sauce over the vegetables.
Serve garnished with almonds or bread crumbs.

WILTED BABY GREENS

*W*hen sautéed with garlic and sesame oil, tender, piquant greens lose their bite and develop mellowness. Young Asian greens work the best, but standard supermarket dark leafy greens will also do. This succulent dish is not only a natural for burgers, but goes well with just about any meal.

4 small servings

2 teaspoons canola oil
3 to 5 large garlic cloves,
   minced
¾ pound baby Asian greens,
   coarsely shredded (see Note)
4 teaspoons tamari
4 teaspoons mirin
   (Japanese rice wine)

Several dashes dark sesame oil,
   to taste
Several dashes balsamic
   vinegar, to taste
Salt (optional)

❶ Heat the canola oil in a large skillet over moderate heat. Cook the garlic until it is golden. Add the greens, tamari, and rice wine. Reduce heat and cook, covered, 5 to 7 minutes or just until the greens are wilted and tender, but retain their color. Remove from heat.

❷ Whisk together the sesame oil and vinegar and pour over the greens. Toss to coat the leaves. Add salt if desired.

➤ *Note:* Use baby bok choy, mizuna mustard greens, and shungiku (edible chrysanthemum). If these are not available, use Swiss or red chard, mustard greens, or thoroughly rinsed spinach. If you are a gardener, you can use young kale, chard, or beet greens.

COUNTRY SALAD

his rustic salad of coarsely chopped vegetables is common throughout southern Europe. To the traditional four-vegetable combination, I have added chick-peas for extra protein. The salad has a Mediterranean accent created by the addition of a generous portion of chopped fresh basil. A perfect counterpoint for all vegetarian burgers, it can be a lunch on its own when served with crostini or garlic bread.

4 side dish servings

1 medium-sized red bell pepper, cored, seeded, and coarsely chopped
¾ pound tomatoes (2 medium), coarsely chopped
1 cup coarsely chopped red or other sweet onion
1 medium cucumber, peeled, seeded, and coarsely chopped

1 cup cooked or canned chick-peas, drained
2 tablespoons chopped fresh basil
¼ to ½ cup Lime Vinaigrette (page 94)

❶ Combine the bell pepper, tomatoes, onion, cucumber, drained chick-peas, and half the basil in a large nonreactive bowl. Cover and leave at room temperature for 15 to 30 minutes. The mixture will form a sauce at the bottom.
❷ Combine the remaining basil with the vinaigrette. Just before serving, stir the vegetables to mix with the sauce at the bottom. Stir in ¼ cup lime vinaigrette, adding more if desired. Mix again thoroughly.

GINGERY TOMATO
SOUP WITH TOFU

*t*his bright red soup with its mellow warmth is a delightful starter for any burger meal.

4 small servings

2½ pounds unpeeled tomatoes, coarsely chopped (see Note)

2 teaspoons minced garlic, or to taste

1½ teaspoons sugar (see Note)

½ teaspoon salt

2 tablespoons olive oil

1 to 2 teaspoons grated ginger root, or to taste

7 ounces firm tofu (½ a 14-ounce carton), drained, rinsed, and cut into ½-inch cubes (optional; see Alternative to Tofu below)

½ teaspoon asafetida powder

¼ teaspoon cumin seeds

1 cup diced onion

GARNISH

Fresh chopped basil, cilantro, or parsley

❶ Place the tomatoes, garlic, and ¼ cup water in a large nonreactive pan over medium-low heat. Cook, covered, until the mixture comes to a low boil. Add the sugar and salt. Reduce heat and simmer, covered, until the tomatoes break down, 12 to 15 minutes. Working in batches, purée the mixture in a blender or food processor. Return to the pan and place over low heat.

❷ Heat 1 tablespoon of the olive oil in a medium skillet over moderate heat. Add the ginger root and cook until it is lightly browned. Add the tofu. Cook until the tofu is lightly browned, a few minutes, gently turning the pieces once. Remove the tofu and ginger root with a slotted spoon and add to the soup.

❸ Heat the remaining 1 tablespoon olive oil in the same skillet over moderate heat. Sprinkle asafetida over the oil. Add the cumin seeds and cook until the seeds turn medium brown. Add the onion. Cook until the onion softens and its edges start to turn brown, about 5 minutes, stirring often. Pour this mixture over the soup. Taste and adjust salt and sugar. Serve garnished with basil or one of the other herbs.

➤ *Note:* For a smoother texture, peel the tomatoes and chop them coarsely. Cook them only for 6 to 10 minutes in Step 1. The sugar counteracts the tartness of commercial tomatoes. Add a little more if necessary, adjusting according to your taste.

➤ **ALTERNATIVE TO TOFU:** If you don't fancy tofu, omit it. Top the dish in this case with sliced hard-boiled eggs (along with the basil or other herbs) if you like.

ZIPPY BUTTERMILK SOUP

his hassle-free soup is perfect for summer meals. It goes well with most vegetarian burgers and is also good on its own as a snack with a couple of warm chapatis and a salad.

2 servings

2 cups low-fat buttermilk
(see Note)
½ cup low-fat plain yogurt
(see Note)
1 tablespoon sugar (see Note)
Salt (optional)

Dash ground red (or cayenne)
pepper, to taste
1 teaspoon canola oil
¼ teaspoon black mustard seeds
GARNISH
Chopped cilantro, basil, or parsley

❶ Place the buttermilk, yogurt, sugar, salt, and red pepper in a bowl and mix well. Taste and adjust the amount of sugar and salt. ❷ Heat the canola oil in a small skillet over moderate heat. Add the mustard seeds and cook until they start to pop. Remove from heat and pour over the buttermilk mixture; stir. Serve immediately or refrigerate for 45 minutes. Garnish with one of the chopped herbs.

➢ *Note:* You can use nonfat buttermilk and nonfat yogurt, but the result will not be as rich and creamy. The sugar is used to reduce the tartness of commercial yogurt. You may need to adjust its amount based on the brand of yogurt.

WINE-GLAZED
MUSHROOMS

hese flavorful mushrooms make a perfect side dish for vegetarian burgers. Fresh shiitake mushrooms work best, although standard fresh mushrooms found in supermarkets will also do. If you are using this recipe for stuffing burgers, chop the mushrooms fine.

4 small servings

1½ tablespoons olive oil
1 cup chopped scallions
½ pound fresh shiitake
    mushrooms, tough stem ends
    trimmed, sliced ½ inch thick
    (or standard supermarket
    mushrooms, sliced ½ inch
    thick)

2 tablespoons mirin (Japanese
    rice wine)
Salt

Heat the olive oil in a medium skillet over moderate heat. Add the scallions and mushrooms. Cook, uncovered, until the mushrooms are softened, 2 to 3 minutes, stirring often. Add the rice wine and cook, uncovered, for 2 to 3 more minutes. Lift the vegetables with a slotted spoon and transfer to a plate, leaving any sauce in the pan. Cook the sauce, uncovered, over moderate heat for a few minutes until it has a thick, syrupy consistency. Remove from heat. Return the vegetables to the skillet and mix well with the sauce. Season to taste with salt.

SAFFRON RICE PILAF

his stunning pilaf, a fragrant combination of basmati rice, saffron, cinnamon, and cardamom, is a perfect accompaniment for vegetarian burgers served as a main course.

3 to 4 side dish servings

1 to 2 tablespoons canola oil
  or butter
½ teaspoon cumin seeds
1 (2-inch) cinnamon stick
4 to 5 whole cardamom pods
2 tablespoons to ¼ cup
  unsalted, raw cashew halves
  (or a mixture of cashews,
  pistachios, and slivered
  almonds to taste)

2 tablespoons golden raisins
1 cup white basmati rice
  (see Note)
¾ teaspoon saffron threads
  mixed with 1 tablespoon
  warm water and allowed to
  stand for 10 minutes
½ cup thawed frozen peas
Salt (optional)

❶ Heat the canola oil or butter in a large saucepan over moderate heat. Add the cumin seeds, cinnamon stick, and cardamom pods. Cook until the cumin seeds start to turn medium brown, stirring often. Add the cashews and raisins and stir to distribute evenly. Stir in the rice. Cook, stirring continuously, for a minute or two until rice is well coated with the oil.

❷ Add 2 cups water and the saffron with its soaking water. Bring to a boil. Reduce heat and simmer, covered, until all the water is absorbed and the rice is tender and fluffy, 10 to 15 minutes. Add the peas during the last 5 minutes of cooking. Let rest, covered, for a few minutes. Before serving, fluff with a fork and season with salt if you like..

➤ *Note:* You can substitute couscous, quinoa, or millet for the rice. Couscous cooks in about the same time as rice. Cook quinoa and millet slightly longer, 15 to 20 minutes.

➤ **MIDDLE EASTERN BUFFET:** If you desire an especially elegant presentation, mound the pilaf in the center of a heated oval platter and sprinkle with cilantro and Caramelized Onion (page 113). Then arrange vegetarian burgers of your choice around the base of the pilaf. Top the pilaf with radish, cucumber, and raw sweet onion slices. Accompany with Cucumber-Basil Raita (page 124), Indian Ketchup (page 119) and Plum Chutney (page 122).

SESAME EGGPLANT STEAKS

hese intensely flavored eggplant steaks acquire a sensuous buttery consistency when oven-roasted. They are marvelous layered on top of any vegetarian burger or as a side dish with most meals.

4 side dish servings

1½ pounds eggplant, cut into
½-inch thick rounds
(if the rounds are greater
than 3 inches in diameter,
cut in half)
Dark sesame oil for brushing

Black salt and freshly ground
pepper (regular salt can
be substituted)
Hoisin sauce for brushing
Plum sauce for brushing

❶ Preheat oven to 450 degrees.

❷ Brush one side of the eggplant pieces generously with sesame oil and dust with salt and pepper. Place the pieces, seasoned side up, on a lightly oiled baking sheet. (Use a flavorless cooking oil such as canola oil or cooking spray.) Bake for 7 to 10 minutes. Turn the pieces, brush lightly with oil and again dust with salt and pepper.

Bake for another 7 to 10 minutes or until the rounds feel soft when pierced with a fork. Turn them and brush with hoisin sauce and plum sauce. Place under the broiler, sauced side up. Broil about 4 inches from the heat for 2 to 5 minutes or just until the sauce is heated. Watch for any signs of burning and remove immediately if the steaks begin to blacken. Best served warm, but is also good served at room temperature.

➤ **VEGETARIAN EGGS BENEDICT:** In this vegetarian version of the hearty breakfast classic, eggplant steaks replace the traditional ham. Spread toasted English muffin with butter (if desired). Place an eggplant steak on top, arrange a poached egg (or a vegetarian burger of your choice) above it, then cover the ensemble with Basil "Mayonnaise" (page 116) or your favorite hollandaise sauce.

CONDIMENTS

*V*egetarian burgers are quite tasty by themselves, but a well-chosen condiment or two can elevate them to another level entirely. Old standbys like mustard and ketchup work well, but selecting from a plethora of such enhancements as chutneys, salsas, or spreads makes every meal a culinary adventure.

On busy days, I opt for a commercial pickle or a flavored mustard. However, when time permits, I prepare condiments from scratch, which enable me to sneak extra fresh fruits, vegetables, and dairy products into a meal. During spring and summer, I work with seasonal fruits like plums and cherries, thickening them to produce rich glazes or savory chutneys redolent of fragrant Indian spices. In winter I rely more on dried fruit relishes or seasoned yogurt sauces, although I continue to make use of whatever fresh fruits and vegetables are available.

Condiments that are thick and spreadable such as mustard or ketchup are spread on the burgers or rolls, but those that are more juicy or runny such as salsas can be served as a relish to be enjoyed by the spoonful between bites. Yogurt-based sauces have the added advantage of increasing the protein content of the meal. Serve them as you would a salsa or, in the case of more substantial varieties, as a separate course on the side.

The condiments in this chapter are inspired by cuisines from around the world. Some are subtle and prefer to work their magic in the background. Others are bold and assertive. All promise to surprise and delight.

READY-MADE
CONDIMENTS

In addition to the usual ketchup, mustard, and barbecue sauce, here's a list of ready-to-use condiments that require little or no preparation.

HOISIN SAUCE. Spread this savory Chinese dipping sauce on top of burgers or on rolls.

INDIAN PICKLES. As an exciting alternative to supermarket pickles, try shopping in Indian groceries for lime, mango, or garlic pickles. These Indian favorites tend to be highly seasoned, so serve them in small portions. Spread a little on top of burgers or serve a dab separately on the side.

MEXICAN SAUCES. Latin American grocery stores are another excellent source of interesting condiments. You'll find shelves filled with chile- and tomato-based sauces, such as fiery chile habanero salsa or smoky hot chipotle salsa.

OLIVES AND CAPERS. Place finely chopped Kalamata (Greek) olives or drained, minced capers on top of burgers instead of, or in addition to, a sauce.

GOAT CHEESE. Spread soft fresh goat cheese on toasted burger buns for a delightful, musky-pungent flavor.

TAHINI MUSTARD

Many varieties of flavored mustards are now available in the market, but you can easily come up with equally interesting versions of your own for a fraction of the cost. Tahini mustard, a robust blend of pungent mustard, crushed garlic, and nutty roasted sesame paste, is a winner with any vegetarian burger.

Makes 1 cup, 6 small servings

¼ cup roasted sesame tahini (preferred over raw sesame tahini)

¼ cup plus 2 tablespoons Dijon mustard

¼ cup freshly squeezed lime juice

1 tablespoon minced garlic

Salt

Place the tahini, ¼ cup plus 1 tablespoon mustard, lime juice, garlic, and ¾ cup water in a blender. Spin until smooth. Transfer to a medium bowl and season to taste with salt. Taste and add the remaining mustard if you like. Stored in the refrigerator in a covered container, this keeps for several days.

APRICOT MUSTARD

this fruity mustard is wonderful with Indian-spiced burgers.

Makes about ¾ cup, 6 small servings

½ cup Dijon mustard

¼ cup plus 1 tablespoon apricot preserves, stirred until smooth

Place the mustard in a medium bowl. Gradually add the apricot preserves, stirring to break the lumps (apricot bits may remain) and tasting as you do. Stop when the mixture tastes good to you.

HONEY-GINGER MUSTARD

f the honey is solid, place it a pan of warm water until it liquefies, about 10 minutes.

Makes about ¾ cup, 6 small servings

½ cup Dijon mustard
¼ cup honey (or to taste)

Ground powdered ginger or
grated fresh ginger root

Place the mustard in a medium bowl. Add the honey gradually, adjusting according to taste. Add ginger to taste.

MAPLE MUSTARD

Makes about ¾ cup, 6 small servings

½ cup Dijon mustard
¼ cup pure maple syrup,
    or to taste

Dash black pepper
    (optional; to taste)

Place the mustard in a medium bowl. Add the maple syrup gradually, adjusting according to taste. Season with black pepper if you like.

PEANUT SAUCE

This jiffy condiment is a wonderful spread for vegetarian burgers. It is also marvelous as a dressing for spinach salads or as a dip for vegetables, either raw or steamed.

Makes 1½ cups, 4 servings

1 cup crunchy peanut butter
3 tablespoons fat-free
   cream cheese
2 tablespoons rice vinegar
4 teaspoons tamari

2 teaspoons sugar
¼ to ½ teaspoon sambal oelek
   or Tabasco to taste
Salt (optional)

Combine the peanut butter, cream cheese, rice vinegar, tamari, and sugar in a large bowl and mix thoroughly. Add 3 tablespoons of water gradually, stirring to make a smooth sauce of spreadable consistency. If it is too thick, add a little more water. (Some recipes call for using this sauce as a filling for burgers. In this case, omit the water from this recipe entirely.) Add sambal oelek (or Tabasco) and salt to taste.

CARAMELIZED
ONION

*t*hese onion slices are excellent served warm on top of vegetarian burgers, or on the side. For an elegant touch, sprinkle them over cooked grains.

Makes ½ cup, enough to garnish 4 burgers

2 tablespoons olive oil
1 cup thinly sliced onion
   (preferably mild, sweet
   onion such as Vidalia,
   Walla Walla, or Maui)

A few dashes sugar

Heat the olive oil in a medium skillet over moderate heat. Add the onion and cook until it is richly browned, 8 to 15 minutes, stirring continuously. Sprinkle sugar over the onion during the last few minutes of cooking. Remove from heat and place between layers of paper towel to absorb any extra oil. You can prepare these onions ahead of time; just reheat in a skillet, stirring in a few drops of water if necessary to prevent sticking. Alternatively, spread on a cookie sheet and reheat in a 325-degree oven for 7 to 10 minutes or until heated through.

➤ **WINE-GLAZED ONION:** A most delicious variation. Proceed as in the recipe above. When the onion turns medium brown, add 2 tablespoons mirin (Japanese rice wine). Cook until the liquid has evaporated, stirring often. Remove from heat and serve warm. You can omit the sugar in this case.

ROASTED GARLIC PURÉE

Spread this aromatic purée on vegetarian burgers for a special taste treat. It's also a winner piled on top of baked sweet potatoes or as a dip for raw or steamed vegetables.

Makes ½ cup, enough to garnish 4 burgers

12 to 15 whole garlic cloves, peeled
½ teaspoon asafetida powder

¼ cup extra-virgin olive oil
Salt

❶ Preheat oven to 450 degrees.

❷ Place the garlic cloves on an ungreased baking sheet. Bake until thoroughly softened, 5 to 15 minutes, depending on the size of the cloves. Remove each clove as it's done. Check often; don't allow them to burn or they will turn bitter. Purée in a blender with the asafetida and olive oil. Season to taste with salt.

TWO-PEPPER SPREAD

his flavorful spread is a combination of roasted bell and jalapeño peppers blended with a small amount of fine olive oil.

Makes 1 cup, enough to garnish 4 burgers

1 large red bell pepper	1 tablespoon extra-virgin
1 whole jalapeño pepper or	olive oil
other fresh chile of choice	Salt
(a red one, if available)	

❶ Preheat the broiler.

❷ Place the bell pepper and the jalapeño under the broiler until their skins are charred, turning them once or twice. The jalapeño will take 3 to 5 minutes and the bell pepper 5 to 7 minutes. Place both in a paper bag and close the top. Let stand for 10 minutes. Remove from the bag. When the peppers are cool to the touch, peel the bell pepper and discard its skin. Remove and discard the stems, seeds, and inner membranes, and chop the flesh coarsely. Do the same for the jalapeño, keeping its flesh separate from that of the bell pepper.

❸ Process the bell pepper flesh in a blender or food processor to a smooth puree. Add the jalapeño flesh, a little at a time, adjusting according to desired hotness, and process again. (If the jalapeño isn't hot, you can add the entire amount of the flesh.) Transfer to a medium bowl. Add the olive oil gradually, mixing in thoroughly with a fork. Season to taste with salt.

TWO-CHEESE
SPREAD

*t*his luscious spread, a combination of fat-free cream cheese
and a small amount of goat cheese, is a snap to prepare. It has the
fresh, tangy flavor of goat cheese with only a fraction of the fat.

Makes 3/4 to 1 cup, 3 to 4 small servings

¼ cup feta or other soft goat or
sheep cheese of choice
½ cup fat-free cream cheese

1 to 2 teaspoons chopped
chives or fresh herb of
choice, to taste

❶ Mash the feta cheese with a fork, adding a teaspoon or two of
water to make it smooth.

❷ Gradually combine the cream cheese with 2 tablespoons water,
stirring with a fork to break up any lumps. Add the softened feta
cheese and herbs and stir again. The mixture should be spreadable.
If it is too thick, work in a little extra water.

BASIL
"MAYONNAISE"

*t*his smashing spread has a fresh herb flavor and a
mayonnaiselike consistency. Best of all, it's fat-free.

Makes ¾ cup, enough to garnish 4 burgers

1 (8-ounce) package fat-free
cream cheese
2 to 3 teaspoons Dijon mustard
(to taste)

2 tablespoons coarsely chopped
fresh basil leaves
Salt

Process all ingredients except salt in a blender or food processor.
Transfer to a medium bowl and season to taste with salt.

MUSHROOM "CREAM" SAUCE

*t*raditional cream sauces, made with half-and-half, are laden with fat and calories. My alternative here is fat-free cream cheese, which has the same smooth creaminess but none of the fat. Spicy sweet hoisin sauce and meaty mushrooms accent this sauce. Fresh shiitake is my preferred mushroom, although standard fresh supermarket mushrooms also yield good results. Ladle the warm sauce over a vegetarian burger of your choice.

Makes 2 cups, 4 servings

¼ cup fat-free cream cheese (about ½ an 8-ounce package)
2 teaspoons to 1 tablespoon hoisin sauce, or to taste
1½ tablespoons canola oil
1 cup minced onion

⅓ pound fresh shiitake mushrooms, tough stem ends removed, sliced ½ inch thick (or fresh cultivated mushrooms, sliced ½ inch thick)
Salt

❶ Place the cream cheese in a medium bowl. Add 2 teaspoons of the hoisin sauce and 3 tablespoons water gradually, stirring to remove any lumps.

❷ Heat the canola oil in a skillet over moderate heat. Add the onion and cook until it is richly browned, 8 to 12 minutes, stirring often. Add the mushrooms and 2 tablespoons water. Reduce heat and simmer, covered, 3 to 5 minutes or just until the mushrooms are tender. Add the cheese-hoisin mixture, stirring to distribute it evenly. Remove from the heat.

❸ Transfer ¼ cup of the vegetables and sauce to a blender container and purée until smooth. Return to the skillet. Cook, uncovered, over low heat until thick and thoroughly heated, a few minutes. Add salt and adjust the amount of hoisin sauce to your taste.

COCONUT SAMBAL

his sambal, or spicy relish, is a savory mélange of apples, sweet onions, and cucumbers, laced with a refreshing mixture of coconut milk and lime juice. It takes only minutes to prepare and provides an appealing crunchy textural accent to burger meals.

Makes 2¾ cups, 4 servings

3 tablespoons coconut milk
2 tablespoons freshly squeezed
   lime juice
1½ teaspoons sugar
¼ teaspoon salt
2 tablespoons chopped cilantro
   (or a combination of
   arugula leaves and parsley)

1 cup thinly sliced mild red or
   other sweet onion
1 cup chopped sweet apple
   (preferably red-skinned), cut
   into ½-inch cubes
½ cup chopped cucumber
   (peeled, seeded, and cut into
   ½-inch cubes)

❶ Mix the coconut milk, lime juice, sugar, salt, and ½ the cilantro (or arugula/parsley mixture) together in a small bowl.
❷ Combine the onion, apple, and cucumber in a large bowl and pour the coconut-lime dressing over it. This can be done several hours ahead of time. Just before serving, stir well to mix the ingredients with the sauce that has accumulated at the bottom. Serve in individual bowls and garnish with the remaining cilantro.
➤ *Stretch-the-Sambal Tip:* The excess sauce at the bottom of the bowl is wonderful the next day as a topping for grains, baked potatoes, or winter squash.

INDIAN KETCHUP

This spicy condiment, inspired by a tomato chutney common throughout Northern India, is a nice change of pace from American ketchup. It is an appropriate accompaniment for all vegetarian burgers.

Makes 2½ cups, 4 servings

1 tablespoon canola oil
½ teaspoon cumin seeds
2 jalapeño peppers or other
  green chiles of choice,
  cored, seeded, and minced
  (or to taste)
¼ teaspoon ground turmeric

2 pounds Roma (plum) or
  regular tomatoes, unpeeled
  and coarsely chopped
Salt
1½ to 2½ tablespoons sugar
½ teaspoon garam masala
1 tablespoon freshly squeezed
  lime juice

❶ Heat the canola oil in a large nonreactive saucepan over moderate heat. Add the cumin seeds and cook until they are medium brown. Add the jalapeños and turmeric and stir until evenly distributed. Reduce heat. Add the tomatoes and cook, covered, until they have softened, about 15 minutes.

❷ Process the mixture, in batches if necessary, in a blender or food processor until smooth. Return to the pan and reheat. Or, if the sauce is still thin, cook, uncovered, until the sauce thickens, an additional 5 to 10 minutes, stirring often. (The timing will vary with the juiciness of the tomatoes.) Season to taste with salt. Add 1½ tablespoons of the sugar. Taste and add the remaining sugar if you like. The chutney should be gently sweet.

❸ Remove from heat. Stir in garam masala and lime juice. Let stand 10 minutes before serving. Best served warm, but can also be served at room temperature. Stored in the refrigerator in a nonreactive container, it will hold for 2 to 3 days.

CHIPOTLE KETCHUP

*P*reparing ketchup is easy, and after tasting this version you'll want to make your own more often. Chipotle ketchup goes well with all vegetarian burgers and is also delicious served as a sauce over pasta.

Makes 2 cups, 4 servings

1½ pounds Roma (plum)
  tomatoes, unpeeled,
  coarsely chopped
½ cup diced onion
¼ cup sugar

2 tablespoons balsamic vinegar
Dash ground chipotle pepper,
  or to taste
Salt

❶ Place the tomatoes, onion, and ¼ cup water in a nonreactive pot. Cover and cook until the mixture comes to a low boil. Reduce heat. Add the sugar, vinegar, and chipotle pepper. Cook, covered, until the tomatoes break down, about 15 minutes. During this period, uncover and stir occasionally, adding a little water if the mixture sticks.

❷ Process the mixture, in batches if necessary, in a blender or food processor until smooth. Season to taste with salt and adjust the amount of sugar and chipotle pepper. The mixture should be quite thick. (If it is still a little watery, return to the pot and cook, uncovered, 5 to 10 minutes or until thickened.) Serve warm or at room temperature. Stored in the refrigerator in a nonreactive container, it keeps for 2 to 3 days.

DATE-RAISIN CHUTNEY

his delightful fruit chutney with an intense taste can be made throughout the year. It goes well with most burgers, but is particularly delicious with nut and seed burgers.

Makes 1½ cups, 3 to 4 servings

12 pitted dates
¼ cup raisins, soaked in hot water to cover for 30 minutes or until soft, drained
1 tablespoon ketchup (or Chipotle Ketchup, on page 119)

1 jalapeño pepper or other green chile of choice, seeded and chopped (or to taste)
1 teaspoon minced ginger root
1 tablespoon tamarind concentrate
¼ teaspoon salt, or more to taste

Process dates, drained raisins, ketchup, jalapeño, ginger root, 1 teaspoon of the tamarind concentrate, ½ cup plus 1 tablespoon water, and salt in a blender or food processor until smooth. Add a little extra water if the mixture is too thick to process. Taste and add extra salt and tamarind to taste if desired.

*d*PLUM CHUTNEY

uring the short season when they are available, fresh plums make a terrific chutney with a complex fruity flavor that cannot be duplicated using dried plums or prunes. Plum chutney is a superb complement to all vegetarian burgers, but is especially luscious with the grain-based ones.   *Makes 3 cups, 6 servings*

2 pounds fresh Italian plums
  (purple, oval–shaped
  variety), unpeeled and pitted
  (see Note)
1 tablespoon coarsely chopped
  ginger root
1 teaspoon quick–cooking
  tapioca (see Note)

2 teaspoons ground cumin
3 tablespoons sugar (or to taste;
  see Note)
¼ teaspoon black salt
  (preferred; or regular salt)
1 teaspoon canola oil
1 whole dried red chile
¼ teaspoon black mustard seeds

❶ Process the plum pulp with its juices and ginger root in a blender or food processor until smooth. Transfer to a large nonreactive pan and add the tapioca and cumin. Cook, uncovered, over medium-low heat until thick and bubbly, about 10 minutes, stirring occasionally. Add the sugar, a little at a time, adjusting according to taste. Add black salt. Remove from heat and set aside.
❷ Heat the canola oil in a small skillet over moderate heat. Add the chile and cook until it blackens. Add the mustard seeds and cook until they start to pop. Immediately pour this mixture over the plum purée; stir. Taste and adjust salt. Serve immediately or refrigerate for 45 minutes. Discard the chile before serving. Stored in the refrigerator in a tightly sealed nonreactive container, the chutney will keep up to 3 days.

➤ *Note:* Don't substitute small Japanese plums for Italian plums in this dish. If the plums are especially juicy, pit them over a large bowl to catch all the drippings. In this case, you'll need 2 teaspoons to 1 tablespoon tapioca to thicken the purée. Adjust the amount of sugar according to the sweetness of the plums. The final result should be gently sweet, although it's a matter of personal taste.

SALSA INTERNATIONAL

his cosmopolitan salsa is a tangy blend of the traditional *Mexican fresh tomato salsa, peppery Italian arugula leaves, and Indian spices. The sauce is versatile enough to be served with any burger, and also makes an outstanding topping for pasta, grains, and baked potatoes.*

Makes 1½ cups, 3 to 4 servings

¼ teaspoon asafetida powder
½ teaspoon ground cumin
3 to 5 large garlic cloves,
  minced (or to taste)
2 tablespoons freshly squeezed
  lime juice
2 tablespoons chopped arugula
  leaves (see Note)

1 pound unpeeled tomatoes,
  seeded and
  coarsely chopped
Black salt (preferred; or
  regular salt)

Combine all ingredients except the salt in a medium nonreactive bowl. Add black salt or regular salt to taste. Let rest for 30 minutes for flavors to develop. Before serving, taste and adjust salt if necessary.

➤*Note:* If arugula is not available, you can substitute watercress. In a pinch use cilantro or parsley, but the taste will not be as interesting.

➤*Stretch-the-Salsa Tip:* If the tomatoes are very juicy, a substantial amount of liquid will accumulate at the bottom of the bowl. Save some of this liquid (by storing in the refrigerator for up to 2 days in a tightly covered nonreactive container) to use as a base for the next batch of salsa. The flavor will be even more intense. Simply add the liquid to your next batch of salsa.

CUCUMBER-BASIL RAITA

aitas are cooling yogurt-based salads, appreciated by Indians at the end of a spicy meal. They are made by adding diced fruits and vegetables to spiced yogurt. I find that a combination of yogurt and buttermilk, rather than yogurt alone, makes for a creamier raita. In this version, cucumber, basil, and raisins combine with the yogurt-buttermilk mixture to yield a raita that has a crunchy texture and a faintly sweet, sharply fresh taste.

The dish goes well with most burgers, but is particularly good with bean and tempeh burgers. Try also with quinoa and steamed butternut squash for a light meal.

Makes 1¼ cups, 2 to 3 servings

½ cup plain nonfat or low-fat yogurt, stirred until smooth
½ cup low-fat buttermilk
Salt
Dash ground red or cayenne pepper (to taste)
3 tablespoons peeled, seeded, and finely minced cucumber

2 tablespoons raisins, soaked in warm water for 30 minutes
1 tablespoon chopped fresh basil leaves
1 teaspoon canola oil
½ teaspoon asafetida powder
¼ teaspoon black mustard seeds

❶ Combine the yogurt, buttermilk, salt, and red pepper in a large bowl and mix well. Add the cucumber, drained raisins, and half the basil.

❷ Heat the canola oil in a small skillet over moderate heat. Sprinkle asafetida over the oil. Add the mustard seeds and cook until they start to pop. Remove from heat. Pour this mixture over the yogurt-buttermilk combination and stir to distribute evenly. Taste and adjust salt. Garnish with the remaining basil. Chill for 45 minutes. Any leftovers can be stored in the refrigerator for a day or two.

CHERRY GLAZE

his fruit glaze with a tart-sweet contrast makes a fine spread for vegetarian burgers. Of the varieties of cherries available, the best for this dish are tart, red cherries, although a mixture of sweet and tart cherries or sweet cherries alone also works. Just adjust the amount of sugar to your taste. This glaze enhances grain- and bean-based burgers and nut burgers. It can also be served alongside grilled vegetables.

Makes 1½ cups, 3 to 4 servings

3 cups pitted tart red cherries
(or sweet cherries or
a combination)
2 tablespoons to ½ cup sugar
(or to taste)

2 tablespoons quick-
cooking tapioca
½ teaspoon almond extract

❶ Place the cherries, 2 tablespoons sugar, and ¼ cup water in a large nonreactive saucepan over medium heat. When the mixture comes to a low boil, reduce heat to medium low. Cook, uncovered, 8 to 10 minutes or until the cherries have broken down. With a slotted spoon remove 1 cup of the cherries, transfer to a medium bowl and reserve. Process the remaining cherries and the accumulated liquid in a blender or food processor until smooth. (Press the cherries in the bowl with the back of a spoon to extract any remaining liquid and add to the blender or processor.)
❷ Return the purée to the pan and add the tapioca. Cook, uncovered, over medium low heat until thickened, 8 to 12 minutes, stirring occasionally. Add the reserved cherries and the almond extract. Taste and adjust sugar. Remove from heat. Serve warm or at room temperature. The glaze can be stored in the refrigerator in a nonreactive container for a day or two.

FRESH HERB PLATE

combination of fresh chopped herbs is delightful served atop vegetarian burgers as a fragrant alternative to shredded lettuce. Arugula, basil, cilantro, and parsley form the basis for the recipe below, but you can substitute other herbs, such as thyme or oregano, according to taste and availability. Consider also young sorrel leaves for an intense lemony flavor, or shiso leaves for their sharp bite. Sprinkle the chopped herbs thickly over the burgers.

Makes ½ cup, 4 small servings

2 tablespoons chopped
   arugula leaves
2 tablespoons chopped fresh
   basil leaves

2 tablespoons chopped cilantro
2 tablespoons chopped parsley

Combine all the ingredients in a medium bowl. Best served immediately, but can be prepared several hours ahead of time and refrigerated.

FIVE FRESH AROMATICS

resh and clean-tasting, this condiment consists of minced onion, ginger root, garlic, jalapeño (or other green chile), and fresh basil or another fresh herb of your choice. Chop the ingredients fine and place in individual bowls (about ¼ cup each) to be sprinkled on top of burgers according to taste.

4 small servings

INDEX